COMPUTER CODING
Projects
FOR KIDS

COMPUTER CODING
Projects
FOR KIDS

HIGHLAND
LIBRARIES

WITHDRAWN

JON WOODCOCK
FOREWORD BY CAROL VORDERMAN

DK UK

Senior editor Ben Morgan
Senior art editor Jacqui Swan
Jacket design development manager Sophia MTT
Jacket editor Claire Gell
Producer, pre-production Gillian Reid
Producer Mary Slater
Managing editor Lisa Gillespie
Managing art editor Owen Peyton Jones
Publisher Andrew Macintyre
Associate publishing director Liz Wheeler
Art director Karen Self
Design director Phil Ormerod
Publishing director Jonathan Metcalf

DK DELHI

Project editor Suefa Lee
Project art editor Parul Gambhir
Editor Sonia Yooshing
Art editor Sanjay Chauhan
Assistant art editor Sonakshi Singh
Jacket designer Suhita Dharamjit
Managing jackets editor Saloni Singh
DTP designer Jaypal Chauhan
Senior managing editor Rohan Sinha
Managing art editor Sudakshina Basu
Pre-production manager Balwant Singh

First published in Great Britain in 2016
by Dorling Kindersley Limited
80 Strand, London WC2R 0RL

A CIP catalogue record for this book
is available from the British Library.
ISBN: 978-0-2412-4133-2

Printed in China

A WORLD OF IDEAS:
SEE ALL THERE IS TO KNOW

www.dk.com

CAROL VORDERMAN MA (CANTAB), MBE, is one of Britain's best-loved TV presenters and is renowned for her skills in mathematics. She has a degree in engineering from the University of Cambridge. Carol has a keen interest in coding and feels strongly that every child should have the chance to learn such a valuable skill. She has hosted numerous TV shows on science and technology, such as *Tomorrow's World* and *How 2*, on the BBC, ITV, and Channel 4. Whether co-hosting Channel 4's *Countdown* for 26 years, becoming the second-best-selling female non-fiction author of the noughties in the UK, or advising Prime Minister David Cameron on mathematics education in British schools, Carol has a passion and devotion to explaining mathematics, science, and technology in an exciting and easily understandable way.

DR JON WOODCOCK MA (OXON) has a degree in physics from the University of Oxford and a PhD in computational astrophysics from the University of London. He started coding at the age of eight and has programmed all kinds of computers, from single-chip microcontrollers to world-class supercomputers. His many projects include giant space simulations, research in high-tech companies, and intelligent robots made from junk. Jon has a passion for science and technology education, giving talks on space and running computer programming clubs in schools. He has worked on many science and technology books, and is the author of DK's *Computer Coding for Kids*, *Computer Coding Games for Kids*, and DK's series of coding workbooks.

Contents

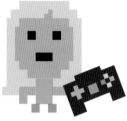

5   SIMULATIONS

7   MINDBENDERS

6   MUSIC AND SOUND

8   WHAT NEXT?

Find out more at:
www.dk.com/computercoding

Foreword

In recent years, interest in coding has exploded. All over the world, schools are adding coding to their curriculums, code clubs are being launched to teach beginners, and adults are returning to college to learn coding skills now considered vital in the workplace. And in homes everywhere, millions of people are learning how to code just for the fun of it.

Fortunately, there's never been a better time to learn how to code. In the past, programmers had to type out every line of code by hand, using obscure commands and mathematical symbols. A single full stop out of place could ruin everything. Today, you can build amazingly powerful programs in minutes by using drag-and-drop coding languages like Scratch™, which is used in this book.

As learning to code has become easier, more people have discovered the creative potential of computers, and that's where this book comes in. *Computer Coding Projects for Kids* is all about using code for creative purposes – to make art, music, animation, and special effects. With a little bit of imagination you can produce dazzling results, from glittering firework displays to kaleidoscope-like masterpieces that swirl and beat in time to music.

If you're completely new to coding, don't worry – the first two chapters will walk you through the basics and teach you everything you need to know to use Scratch. The later chapters then build on your skills, showing you how to create interactive artworks, life-like simulations, mind-bending optical illusions, and some great games.

Learning something new can sometimes feel like hard work, but I believe you learn faster when you're having fun. This book is based on that idea, so we've tried to make it as much fun as possible. We hope you enjoy building the projects in this book as much as we enjoyed making them.

CAROL VORDERMAN

On your marks...
get set... CODE!

What is coding?

Creative computers

Computers are everywhere and are used in all sorts of creative ways. But to really join in the fun, you need to take control of your computer and learn how to program it. Programming puts a world of possibilities at your fingertips.

Think like a computer

Programming, or coding, simply means telling a computer what to do. To write a program you need to think like a computer, which means breaking down a task into a series of simple steps. Here's how it works.

▷ **A simple recipe**
Imagine you want a friend to bake a cake, but your friend has no idea how to cook. You can't simply give them an instruction like "make a cake" – they won't know where to start. Instead, you need to write a recipe, with simple steps like "break an egg", "add the sugar", and so on. Programming a computer is a bit like writing a recipe.

Easy peasy!

Recipe

◁ **Step by step**
Now imagine you want to program a computer to create a painting like the one shown here, with coloured circles overlapping each other at random. You have to turn the job of painting the picture into a kind of recipe, with steps the computer can follow. It might look something like this:

Recipe

Ingredients

1. Ten circles of various sizes

2. Seven colours

Instructions

1. Clear the screen to create a white background.

2. Repeat the following ten times:

    a) Pick a random place on the screen.

    b) Pick one of the circles randomly.

    c) Pick one of the colours randomly.

    d) Draw a see-through copy of the circle at that place in that colour.

▷ Computer language

Although you can understand the recipe for a painting or a cake, a computer can't. You need to translate the instructions into a special language that the computer can understand – a programming language. The one used in this book is called Scratch.

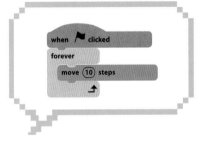

Worlds of imagination

There isn't a single creative field in the world that hasn't been touched by computers. In this book, you'll get to make lots of great projects that will fire your imagination and make you think and code creatively.

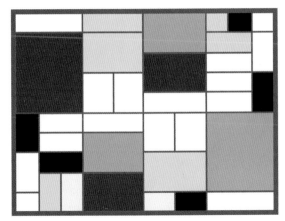

Computers can be programmed to create original works of art.

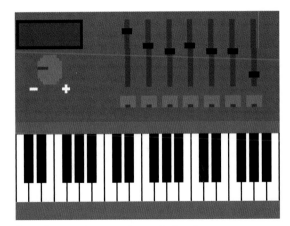

Sound programs can mix musical and other sound effects in any combination.

Building games programs is just as much fun as playing them, especially when you make all the rules.

Special effects and dramatic scenery in films are often created in graphics programs.

Programming languages

To tell a computer what to do, you need to speak the right kind of language: a programming language. There are lots to choose from, ranging from easy ones for beginners, like the one in this book, to complex languages that take years to master. A set of instructions written in any programming language is called a program.

Popular languages

There are more than 500 different programming languages, but most programs are written in just a handful of these. The most popular languages use English words, but lines of code look very different from English sentences. Here's how to get a computer to say "Hello!" on screen in just a few of today's languages.

Hello!

▷ **C**

The C programming language is often used for code that runs directly on a computer's hardware, such as the Windows operating system. C is good for building software that needs to run fast and has been used to program space probes.

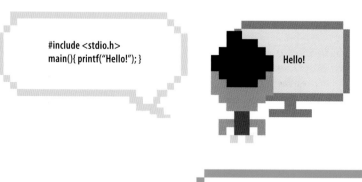

```
#include <stdio.h>
main(){ printf("Hello!"); }
```

Hello!

▷ **C++**

This complicated language is used to build large, commercial programs such as word processors, web browsers, and operating systems. C++ is based on C, but with extra features that make it better for big projects.

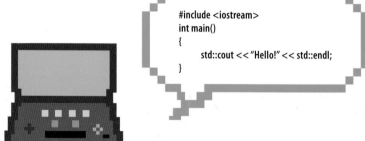

```
#include <iostream>
int main()
{
        std::cout << "Hello!" << std::endl;
}
```

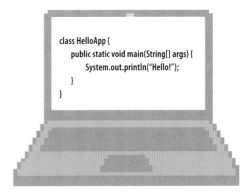

△ **Scratch**

Beginners often start with simple programming languages such as Scratch. Instead of typing out code, you build scripts with ready-made coding blocks.

△ **Java**

Java code is designed to work on all types of devices, from mobile phones and laptops to games consoles and supercomputers. Minecraft is written in Java.

△ **Python**

Python is a very popular, all-purpose language. The lines of code are shorter and simpler than in other languages, making it easier to learn. Python is a great language to learn after Scratch.

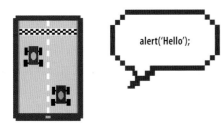

△ **JavaScript**

Programmers use JavaScript to create interactive features that run on websites, such as advertisements and games.

▪▪ LINGO

Code words

Algorithm A set of instructions that are followed to perform a particular task. Computer programs are based on algorithms.

Bug A mistake in a program. They are called bugs because the first computers had problems when insects got stuck in their circuits.

Code Computer instructions written in a programming language are often called code. Coding is programming.

How Scratch works

This book shows you how to build some cool projects using the Scratch programming language. Programs are made by dragging together ready-made instruction blocks to control colourful characters called sprites.

Sprites

Sprites are the objects shown on the screen. Scratch comes with a huge selection of sprites – such as elephants, bananas, and balloons – but you can also draw your own. Sprites can perform all sorts of actions, like moving, changing colour, and spinning round.

I'm a sprite!

Sprites can move around.

Sprites can play sounds and music.

Sprites can deliver messages on the screen.

Blocks and scripts

Scratch's multicoloured instruction blocks tell sprites what to do. Each sprite gets its instructions from stacks of Scratch blocks called scripts. Each instruction block is acted out in turn from the top to the bottom. Here's a simple script for this vampire sprite.

▽ **Creating scripts**

The blocks that make a script are dragged together using a computer mouse. They lock together like jigsaw pieces. Blocks come in colour-coded families to help you find the correct block easily. For example, all the purple blocks change a sprite's appearance.

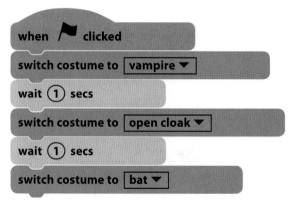

A typical Scratch project

A Scratch project is made up of sprites, scripts, and sounds, which work collectively to create action on the screen. The area where you see the action is called the stage. You can add a background picture called a backdrop to the stage.

The red button stops a program.

The green flag starts the program.

▷ **Green for go!**
Starting, or "running", a program brings to life the scripts you've built. In Scratch, clicking the green flag runs all the scripts in the project. The red button stops the scripts so you can continue working on your code.

The stage and lights are part of the backdrop (background picture).

The dancing dinosaurs and ballerina are sprites controlled by their own scripts.

▽ **Scripts work together**
A project usually has several sprites, each with one or more scripts. Each script creates just a part of the action. This script makes a sprite chase the mouse-pointer around the stage.

The "forever" block makes the blocks inside repeat.

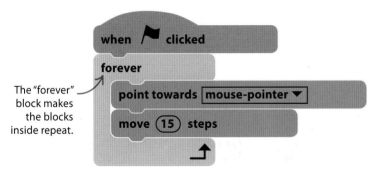

Reading Scratch

Scratch is designed to be easily understood. The action performed by each block is written on it, so you can usually work out what a script does just by reading through it.

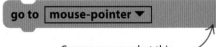

Can you guess what this block makes sprites do?

Getting Scratch 2.0

To build the projects in this book and to make your own, you need access to the Scratch 2.0 software on your computer. Just follow these simple instructions.

This book uses Scratch 2.0!

Online and offline Scratch

If your computer is always connected to the internet, it's best to run Scratch online. If not, you need to download and install the offline version.

ONLINE

Visit the Scratch website at **http://scratch.mit.edu** and click on "Join Scratch" to create an account with a username and password. You'll need an email address too.

Online Scratch runs in your web browser, so just go to the Scratch website and click on "Create" at the top of the screen. The Scratch interface will open.

You don't have to worry about saving your work as the online version of Scratch saves projects automatically.

Online Scratch should work on Windows, Mac, and Linux computers (but not on Raspberry Pi) as long as you have a modern web browser.

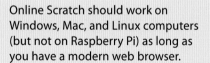

OFFLINE

Visit the Scratch website at **http://scratch.mit.edu/scratch2download/** and follow the instructions to download and install Scratch on your computer.

Scratch will appear as an icon on your desktop, just like any other installed program. Double-click on the Scratch cat icon to get going.

You'll need to save your project by clicking on the File menu and selecting "Save". Scratch will ask you where to save your work – check with the computer's owner.

Offline Scratch works well on Windows and OS X, but often runs into trouble on Linux computers.

Versions of Scratch

The projects in this book need Scratch 2.0 and won't work properly on older versions. If Scratch is already installed on your computer then consult the pictures below if you're not sure which version it is.

▽ **Scratch 1.4**

In the older version of Scratch, the stage appears on the right. You'll need to install Scratch 2.0. Note that when this book was written, Scratch 1.4 was the only version that could run on the Raspberry Pi.

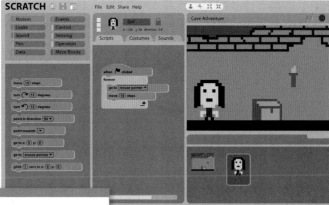

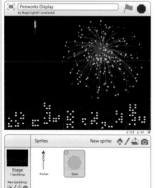

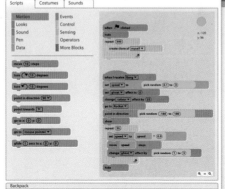

◁ **Scratch 2.0**

In the latest version of Scratch, released in 2013, the stage is on the left and there are many more blocks and features than in the older version. Key changes include the addition of clones, a better paint editor, and the backpack, where you can save scripts, sprites, and other useful things.

■·■ EXPERT TIPS

Mouse-pointers

Scratch needs some accurate mouse-work, which is easier to do with a computer mouse than a touchpad. In this book, you'll often be instructed to right-click something with your computer mouse. If your mouse only has one button, you can hold down the shift or control key on your keyboard as you click.

The Scratch interface

This is Scratch mission control. The tools for building scripts are on the right, while the stage to the left shows you what's going on as your project runs. Don't be afraid to explore!

Change language

Menus

Cursor tools

SCRATCH   File ▼   Edit ▼   Tips

Dino Dance Party
by PartyPeople555 (unshared)

Click here for a full-screen view of your project.

The Stage
This is where the action happens. When you run your project, the stage is where all the sprites appear, moving and interacting as they follow their scripts.

x: 153   y: -0

Sprites   New sprite:

Stage
1 backdrop

New backdrop:

Dinosaur1   Dinosaur2   Dinosaur3   Ballerina

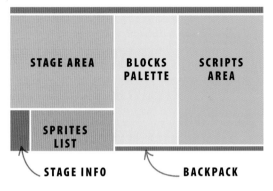

STAGE AREA	BLOCKS PALETTE	SCRIPTS AREA
SPRITES LIST		

STAGE INFO   BACKPACK

△ **Naming the parts**
While using this book you'll need to know what's where in the Scratch window. Shown here are the names of the different areas. The tabs above the blocks palette open up other areas of Scratch to edit sounds and sprite costumes.

Use these symbols to change the backdrop.

A blue box highlights the selected sprite.

Sprites list
Every sprite used in a project is shown here. Click on a sprite to see its scripts in the scripts area.

Click these symbols to add new sprites.

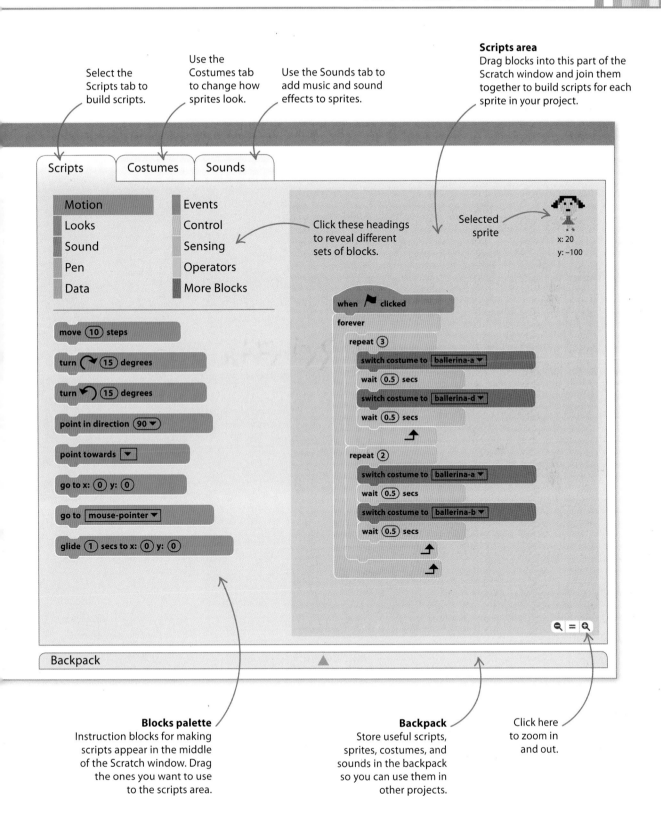

Select the Scripts tab to build scripts.

Use the Costumes tab to change how sprites look.

Use the Sounds tab to add music and sound effects to sprites.

Scripts area
Drag blocks into this part of the Scratch window and join them together to build scripts for each sprite in your project.

Scripts Costumes Sounds

Motion
Looks
Sound
Pen
Data

Events
Control
Sensing
Operators
More Blocks

Click these headings to reveal different sets of blocks.

Selected sprite

x: 20
y: −100

move 10 steps

turn 15 degrees

turn 15 degrees

point in direction 90

point towards

go to x: 0 y: 0

go to mouse-pointer

glide 1 secs to x: 0 y: 0

when clicked
forever
repeat 3
switch costume to ballerina-a
wait 0.5 secs
switch costume to ballerina-d
wait 0.5 secs

repeat 2
switch costume to ballerina-a
wait 0.5 secs
switch costume to ballerina-b
wait 0.5 secs

Backpack

Blocks palette
Instruction blocks for making scripts appear in the middle of the Scratch window. Drag the ones you want to use to the scripts area.

Backpack
Store useful scripts, sprites, costumes, and sounds in the backpack so you can use them in other projects.

Click here to zoom in and out.

Types of project

This book has a wide range of fun Scratch projects. Don't worry if you haven't used Scratch before or you're not an expert – the "Getting started" chapter is there to help you. Here's a handy guide to the projects in this book.

Cat Art (p.26)

Dino Dance Party (p.34)

Animal Race (p.48)

Ask Gobo (p.60)

△ **Getting started**

Work your way through these easy projects to learn how to use Scratch. Each project introduces important new ideas, so don't skip any if you're a beginner. By the end of the chapter, you'll have mastered the basics of Scratch.

Funny Faces (p.70)

Birthday Card (p.82)

Spiralizer (p.94)

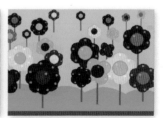

Fantastic Flowers (p.106)

◁ **Art**

Artists love finding new ways to create art, and computers give them tools that even Leonardo da Vinci couldn't have dreamed of. Make a birthday card, spin spectacular spirals, and cover your world with flowers.

▷ **Games**

Game design is one of the most creative areas of coding. Game makers are always looking for imaginative new ways to challenge players or tell stories. The projects in this chapter challenge you to steer a sprite through a twisty tunnel or clean virtual splats off a dirty computer screen.

Tunnel of Doom (p.122)

Window Cleaner (p.134)

Virtual Snow (p.144)

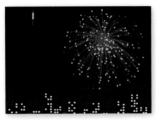

Firework Display (p.154)

Fractal Trees (p.162)

Snowflake Simulator (p.172)

△ Simulations

Give a computer the correct information and it can mimic, or simulate, the way things work in the real world. This chapter shows you how to simulate falling snow, sparkling fireworks, the growth of trees, and the shapes of snowflakes.

Sprites and Sounds (p.182)

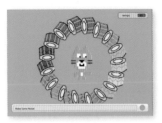

Drumtastic (p.190)

◁ Music and sound

While early computers struggled to make simple beeps, modern computers can reproduce every instrument in an orchestra. Try out these two treats for your ears. The first one matches sound effects with silly animations, and the second one puts a digital drum kit at your fingertips.

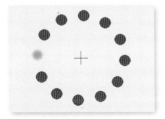

The Magic Spot (p.200)

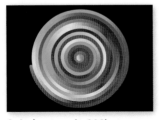

Spiral-o-tron (p.208)

◁ Mindbenders

Making images move in clever ways can fool the eye into seeing amazing patterns and optical illusions. Try these mindbending, spinning-pattern projects.

EXPERT TIPS

Perfect projects

Every project in this book is broken down into easy steps – read each step carefully and you'll sail through them all. The projects tend to get more complicated later in the book. If you find a project isn't doing what it should do, go back a few steps and check the instructions again carefully. If you still have problems, ask an adult to check with you. Once you've got a project working, don't be afraid to change the code and try out your own ideas.

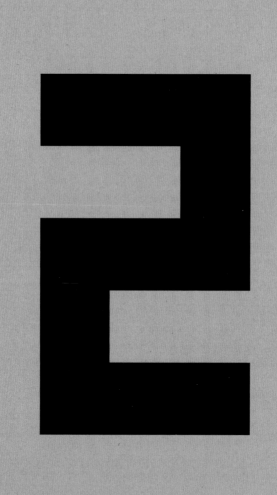

Getting started

Cat Art

Find your feet in Scratch by making some super-simple art with Scratch's cat sprite – the mascot of the Scratch project. This project turns the cat into a kind of multicoloured paintbrush. You can use the same trick to paint with any sprite.

Click here to make the project fill your screen.

Type the name of your project here.

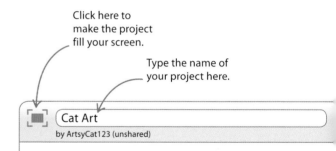

Cat Art
by ArtsyCat123 (unshared)

How it works

This simple project lets you use a computer mouse to paint multicoloured cat art. Wherever you drag the mouse, a rainbow trail of cats is left behind. Later on you'll see how to add other effects.

△ **Follow the mouse**
First you'll make a script to use the mouse-pointer to move the cat sprite around the stage.

△ **Changing colour**
Next you'll add blocks to the script to make the cat change its colour.

△ **Making copies**
Then you'll use the "stamp" block to make a trail of copies appear on the stage.

△ **Going wild**
There are lots of crazy effects you can try out on the cat once you start experimenting.

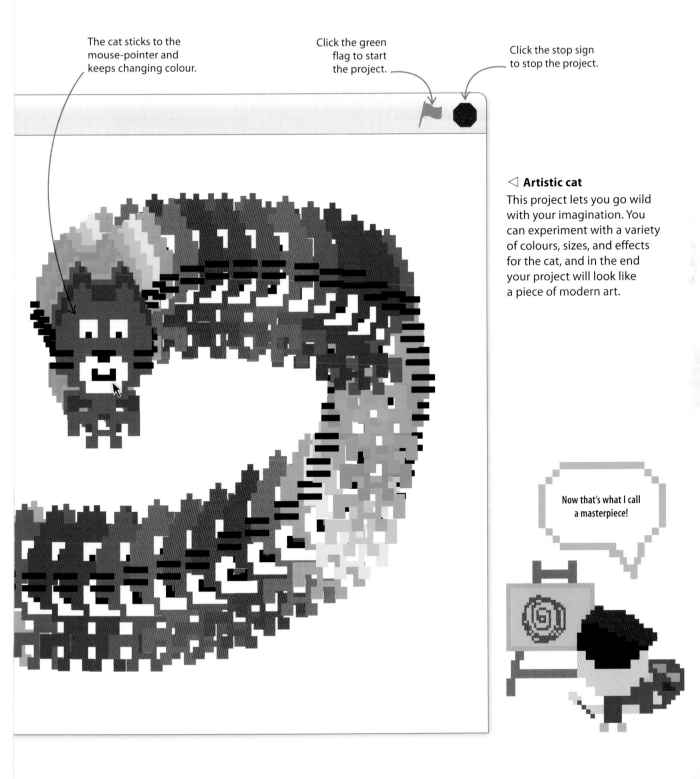

The cat sticks to the mouse-pointer and keeps changing colour.

Click the green flag to start the project.

Click the stop sign to stop the project.

◁ **Artistic cat**
This project lets you go wild with your imagination. You can experiment with a variety of colours, sizes, and effects for the cat, and in the end your project will look like a piece of modern art.

Now that's what I call a masterpiece!

Multicoloured cats

Scratch is packed full of ways to make art. The simple script changes here will send your cat straight to the art gallery.

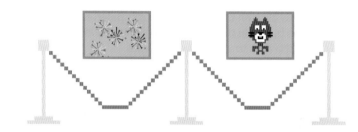

8 Click on Looks at the top of the blocks palette and find the "change colour effect by (25)" block. Drag this into the loop in your script so it looks like this.

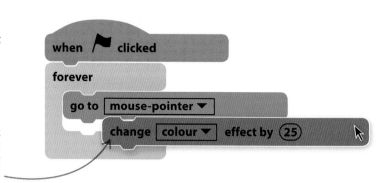

What do you think will happen when you run this new version of the script?

9 Click the green flag to run the new version of the project. The cat now changes colour from moment to moment. Every time the loop repeats the "change colour effect by" block, the sprite shifts in colour a little.

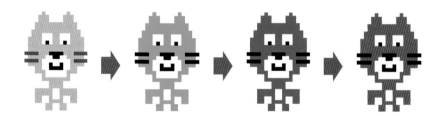

10 Now comes the moment to make some art. We need just one more block. Click on Pen in the blocks palette and you'll see a selection of green blocks. Drag a "stamp" block into the loop so your script looks like this:

Let's make some art!

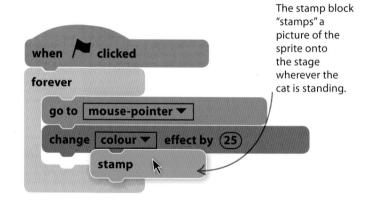

The stamp block "stamps" a picture of the sprite onto the stage wherever the cat is standing.

11 Next, run the project again by clicking the green flag. The cat will leave a trail of multicoloured cats behind it. What an artistic sprite!

Each cat in the trail is put there by the stamp block.

12 You'll find that the stage soon fills up with cats, but don't worry, as you can add a script to wipe it clean at the press of a button. Choose Pen in the blocks palette and look for the "clear" block. Drag it into the scripts area but keep it separate from the first script. Then click on Events and add a brown "when space key pressed" block. Run the project and see what happens when you press the space-bar.

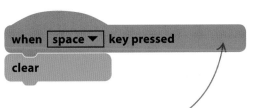

This header block starts the script when the chosen key is pressed on the keyboard.

EXPERT TIPS

Full screen

To see projects at their best, you can simply click the full-screen button just above the stage to hide the scripts and just show the results. There's a similar button to shrink the stage and reveal the scripts again from full-screen mode.

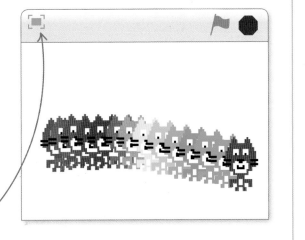

Click here to see your project fill the screen.

If you use the offline version of Scratch, don't forget to save your work from time to time.

Hacks and tweaks

There are lots of ways to change how the cat looks, and you can use them to create some startling visual effects. Below are a few tips, but feel free to try your own experiments.

▽ **Try this for size**

Add these two scripts to the cat to make it bigger or smaller when you press the up or down arrow keys.

Click on the triangle to choose the correct key from a drop-down list.

when [up arrow ▼] key pressed

change size by (10)

when [down arrow ▼] key pressed

change size by (−10)

Positive numbers make the cat bigger and negative numbers make it smaller.

• • •   **TRY THIS**

Crazy cat

Try growing your cat until it fills the stage. Press the space-bar to clear all the other cats, leave the computer mouse alone and hold down the down arrow. A succession of ever-smaller cats will appear inside each other, creating a multicoloured, cat-shaped tunnel!

▽ **Smooth changes**

Don't be afraid to experiment with the numbers and settings in Scratch commands. You don't have to change the cat's colour effect by 25 each time. The lower the number, the more slowly the colour will change, like in this rainbow.

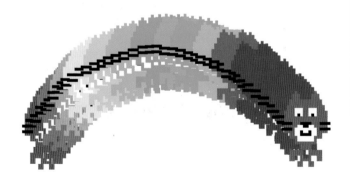

when ⚑ clicked

forever

    go to [mouse-pointer ▼]

    change [colour ▼] effect by (1)

    stamp

Set this number to 1 for a smoother colour change.

▽ Special effects

There are lots of other effects to try besides simple colour changes. Try adding another "change" block to the main script. Click the drop-down menu and try the other effects to see what they do.

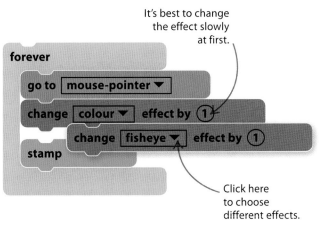

It's best to change the effect slowly at first.

Click here to choose different effects.

▽ At your fingertips

To give yourself more control over effects while painting with the cat, you can trigger scripts with any keys you choose. You could create a whole keyboard full of weird cat changes, including the ghost effect shown here.

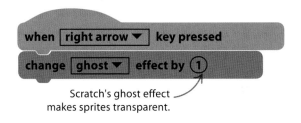

Scratch's ghost effect makes sprites transparent.

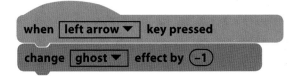

▽ Cleaning up

Things can get messy with effects, so add a "clear graphic effects" block to the script below. This runs when you press the space-bar to clear the stage.

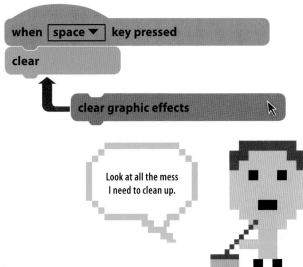

Look at all the mess I need to clean up.

EXPERT TIPS

Loops

Almost all computer programs contain loops. These are useful as they let a program go back and repeat a set of instructions, which keeps scripts simple and short. The "forever" block creates a loop that goes on forever, but other types of loops can repeat an action a fixed number of times. You'll meet all sorts of clever loops in projects later in the book.

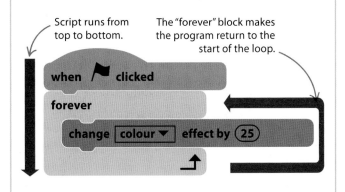

Script runs from top to bottom.

The "forever" block makes the program return to the start of the loop.

Dino Dance Party

Brush off your dancing shoes and join the dinosaur's dance party! Who will you invite? There will be music, a light show, and dance moves galore. Dance routines are just like computer programs – you just follow the steps in order.

Click this icon to make the game fill your screen.

Type the name of the project here.

Dino Dance Party
by PartyPeople555 (unshared)

How it works

Each sprite has one or more scripts that program its dance moves. Some simply turn from side to side, but others glide across the dance floor or perform more varied moves. You can add as many dancers as you like.

◁ **Dinosaur**
After you've created a dancing dinosaur, you can duplicate this sprite to make a group of dinosaurs dancing in rhythm.

The "spotlight-stage" backdrop sets the scene for the dance party.

◁ **Ballerina**
To add a touch of class, the ballerina will perform a more complicated dance routine.

The disco lights change colour several times a second.

Click the green flag to start the project.

Click the stop sign to stop the project.

By switching between different poses, the sprites appear to dance.

Let's party!

Dancing dinosaur

Scratch has lots of ready-made sprites for your project in the sprite library. Many of the sprites have several "costumes", each showing the sprite in a different pose. If you make a sprite switch costumes quickly, it looks like it's moving.

1 First start a fresh Scratch project. From the main Scratch website, click on Create at the top. If a Scratch project is already open, click on the File menu above the stage and select "New".

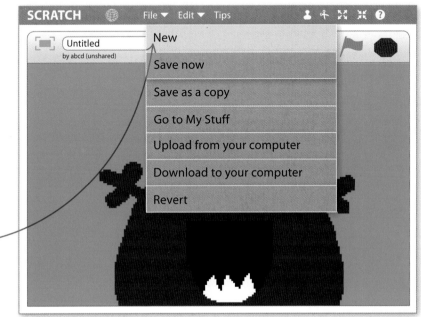

Clicking on "New" will save an existing project before starting a fresh one.

2 New projects always start with the cat sprite, but we don't need it this time. To delete it, right-click on the cat (or control/shift-click on a one button mouse) and select "delete". The cat will disappear.

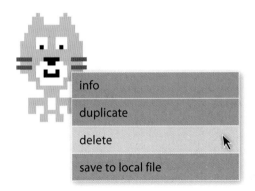

3 To load a new sprite, click on the small sprite symbol ♣ in the sprites list just below the stage. A window with a huge selection of sprites will open. Choose Dinosaur1 and click "OK". Dinosaur1 will now appear on the stage and in the sprites list.

Click here to load a new sprite.

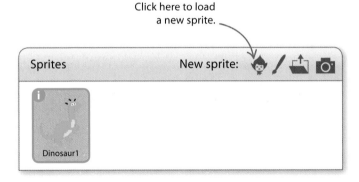

4 Make this simple script for Dinosaur1. Look carefully and you'll see the script runs when the space-bar is pressed – not when the green flag is clicked.

You can find brown blocks by clicking on Events in the blocks palette.

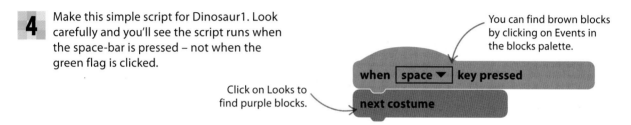

when space ▼ key pressed

Click on Looks to find purple blocks.

next costume

5 Look at the dinosaur on the stage and press the space-bar. Every time you press it, the dinosaur will change its pose. It's still the Dinosaur1 sprite, but the way it looks keeps changing. Each different pose is called a costume and can be used to make a sprite appear to do different things.

Each pose is a different costume belonging to the dinosaur sprite.

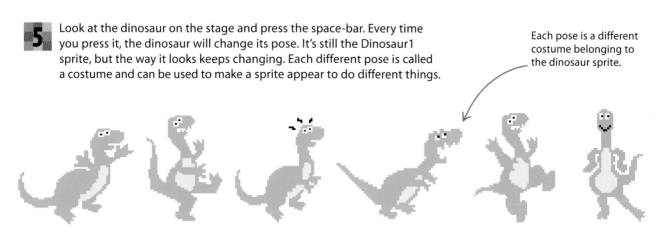

6 Click on the Costumes tab at the top of the blocks palette to see all the dinosaur's costumes. Press the space-bar to trigger the "next costume" block and you'll see the blue outline move to each costume in turn as it's selected.

Each costume has a different name.

This part of the Scratch window is called the paint editor. Later on you'll find out how to use it to create your own sprites and backdrops.

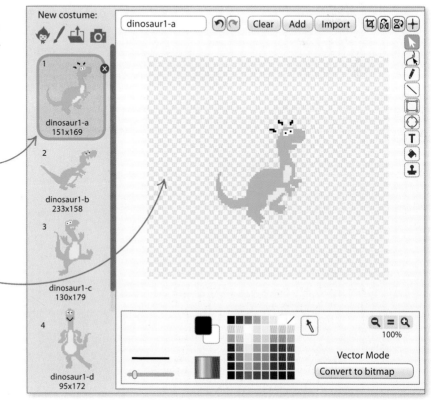

Dance steps

By using loops you can make the dinosaur change its costume repeatedly, making it appear to move. Changing pictures quickly to give the illusion of movement is called animation.

7 Click on the Scripts tab at the top of the Scratch window to go back to the dinosaur's scripts and add this script. Before you try it, read through the script and see if you can figure out what it does.

8 Click the green flag above the stage to run the script. You'll see the dinosaur move wildly as it loops through all its costumes at high speed. To make a neater dance, the next step will limit the number of costumes to just two.

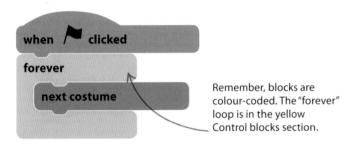

Remember, blocks are colour-coded. The "forever" loop is in the yellow Control blocks section.

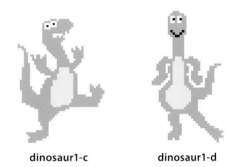

dinosaur1-c   dinosaur1-d

9 Remove the "next costume" block from the loop and replace it with the blocks shown here. The new script switches between two costumes and slows everything down with some "wait" blocks. Run the project again by clicking the green flag – the dinosaur should now dance more sensibly.

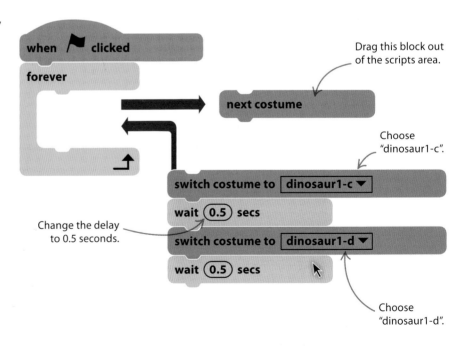

Drag this block out of the scripts area.

Choose "dinosaur1-c".

Change the delay to 0.5 seconds.

Choose "dinosaur1-d".

```
when [flag] clicked
forever
  next costume
  switch costume to [dinosaur1-c ▼]
  wait (0.5) secs
  switch costume to [dinosaur1-d ▼]
  wait (0.5) secs
```

10 To add more dancing dinosaurs to the party you can simply copy the first dinosaur. Right-click on the dinosaur in the sprites list and choose "duplicate" from the pop-up menu. A new dinosaur will appear in the sprites list.

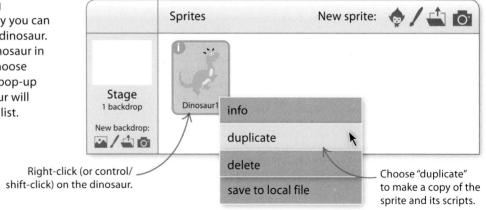

Right-click (or control/ shift-click) on the dinosaur.

Choose "duplicate" to make a copy of the sprite and its scripts.

11 Make another copy so that there are three dinosaurs in total. Click on the dinosaurs on the stage and drag each one to a good spot. Run the project. Since they all have the same script, they'll all do the same dance at the same time.

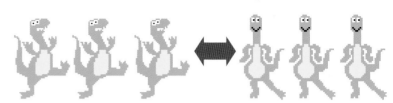

Setting the scene

The dinosaurs are dancing, but the room's a bit boring. Follow the next steps to add some decorations and music. You'll need to make some changes to the stage. Although it isn't a sprite, it can still have its own scripts.

12 First, a change of scenery. The picture on the stage is called a backdrop and you can load new ones. Look at the bottom left of the screen and click on the backdrop symbol to the left of the sprites list.

13 Select "spotlight-stage" from the backdrops library and click "OK". This backdrop will now appear behind the dancers.

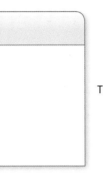

Click this symbol to add a backdrop.

The "spotlight-stage" backdrop sets the mood of the party.

14 Now click on the Scripts tab at the top of the screen to add a script to the stage – each sprite can have its own scripts and so can the stage.

Click here to show the scripts area.

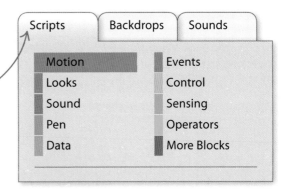

15 Add this script to make the disco lights flash. Then click the green flag to run the project – it should look like a real disco. You can experiment with the time in the "wait" block to make the lights flash faster or slower if you want.

This block only changes the backdrop colours. It does not affect the other sprites.

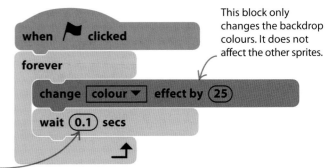

Adjust the number here to change how fast the lights flash.

16 Now it's time to add some music. Click on the Sounds tab, which is next to the Scripts tab at the top. Then click on the speaker symbol 🔊 to open Scratch's sound library. Select "dance around" and click "OK" to load it into the stage's list of sound clips.

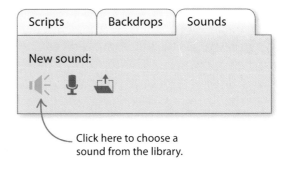

Click here to choose a sound from the library.

17 Click on the Scripts tab again and add this new script to play the music in a loop. Click the green flag to run the project again. The music should play. You now have a real party on your hands!

Don't forget to click the full-screen symbol above the stage to see me at my best.

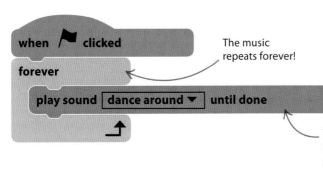

The music repeats forever!

This block plays the whole tune before the script goes back to the start.

Get a move on!

The dinosaurs are throwing some wicked shapes, but they're not moving around the dance floor much. You can fix that with some new scripts that use Scratch's "move" block.

Click here to see Dinosaur2's scripts.

18 First, click on Dinosaur2 in the sprites list to show its scripts in the scripts area.

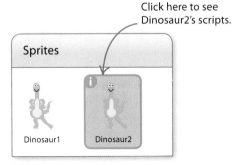

19 Next, add this extra script. To find the dark blue blocks, click Motion at the top of the blocks palette. What do you think the new script does?

```
when ⚑ clicked
forever
    move 10 steps
    if on edge, bounce
```

These aren't actual dinosaur steps, they're Scratch's way of measuring distances.

Add this block to turn the dinosaur round at the stage's edge.

20 Now click the green flag and both of Dinosaur2's scripts will run at the same time. The sprite will move all the way across the stage and then turn around and dance back. But you'll notice that it dances back upside down!

21 To prevent the blood rushing to the dinosaur's tiny brain, click on the blue "i" symbol next to the sprite in the sprites list. This reveals extra information about the sprite.

Click here.

Dinosaur2

22 An information box will pop up. Change "rotation style" to the double arrow and watch the dinosaur dance. See what happens if you click the other rotation styles. You now have the power to choose whether the dinosaur dances on its head or not!

Click here to go back to the sprites list.

Select the double arrow to keep the dinosaur upright.

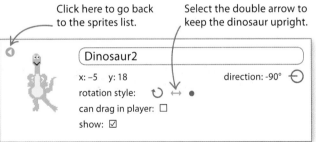

Dinosaur2

x: −5   y: 18   direction: -90°

rotation style: ↻ ↔ •

can drag in player: ☐

show: ☑

Keyboard control

Ever dreamed of taking control of your very own dinosaur? The next script will give you keyboard control of Dinosaur3's movements: you'll be able to move the dinosaur across the stage with the right and left arrow keys.

23 Click on Dinosaur3 in the sprites list so you can edit its scripts.

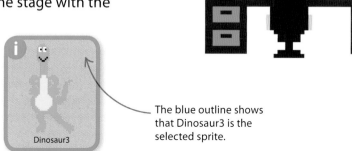

The blue outline shows that Dinosaur3 is the selected sprite.

24 Add this script to the scripts area. It's quite complicated, so make sure you get everything in the right place. The "if then" block is in the yellow Control blocks section. It's a special block that chooses whether or not to run the blocks inside it by asking a question. Take care to ensure that both "if then" blocks are inside the "forever" loop and not inside each other.

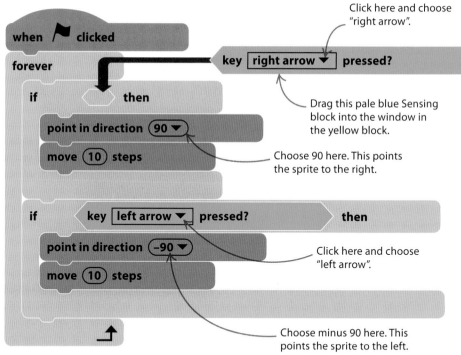

Click here and choose "right arrow".

Drag this pale blue Sensing block into the window in the yellow block.

Choose 90 here. This points the sprite to the right.

Click here and choose "left arrow".

Choose minus 90 here. This points the sprite to the left.

25 Before you run the script, read through it carefully and see if you can understand how it works. If the right arrow key is pressed, blocks that make the sprite point right and move are run. If the left arrow key is pressed, blocks that make the sprite point left and move are run. If neither is pressed, no blocks are run and the dinosaur stays put. Repeat step 22 to stop Dinosaur3 from turning upside down.

EXPERT TIPS

Making choices

You make choices all the time. If you're hungry, you decide to eat; if not, you don't. Computer programs can also make choices between different options. One way to make them do this is to use an "if then" instruction, which is used in lots of programming languages. In Scratch, the "if then" block includes a statement or a question and only runs the code inside the block if the statement is true (or the answer is yes).

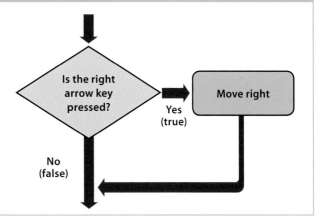

Is the right arrow key pressed?

Yes (true)

Move right

No (false)

Add a ballerina

The dinosaurs are dancing, but it's not much of a party without some friends. A ballerina is going to join the fun and will do a routine. Her scripts will show you how to create more complicated dance routines.

26 Click on the sprite symbol ♟ in the sprites list and load the ballerina. Then use your mouse to drag the sprite to a good spot on the stage. To give the ballerina some scripts, make sure she's selected in the sprites list – the selected sprite has a blue outline.

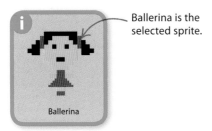

Ballerina is the selected sprite.

Ballerina

27 You can see all the costumes of a sprite by clicking on the Costumes tab when the sprite is selected. The ballerina has four costumes, and switching between them will make her dance a beautiful ballet.

| Scripts | Costumes | Sounds |

New costume:

ballerina-a

1

ballerina-a
61x10

2

ballerina-b
66x81

Each costume has a unique name.

28 Using the names of the different costumes, you can design a dance routine for the ballerina, like the one shown here. Each step in the dance will become an instruction block in the code.

Costume ballerina-a then ballerina-d, repeated three times.

29 Build this script to create the ballerina's first dance. There's no "forever" loop – instead, the script uses a "repeat" loop that runs a fixed number of times before moving on to the next block. Run the project to see her perform the dance routine.

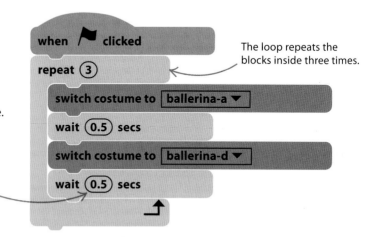

The loop repeats the blocks inside three times.

To set the delay time, click on the window and type 0.5.

```
when 🏴 clicked
repeat 3
    switch costume to ballerina-a ▼
    wait 0.5 secs
    switch costume to ballerina-d ▼
    wait 0.5 secs
```

⸬ LINGO

Algorithms

An algorithm is a series of simple, step-by-step instructions that together carry out a particular task. In this project, we converted the ballerina's dance routine (an algorithm) into a program. Every computer program has an algorithm at its heart. Programming is translating the steps of the algorithm into a computer programming language that the computer understands.

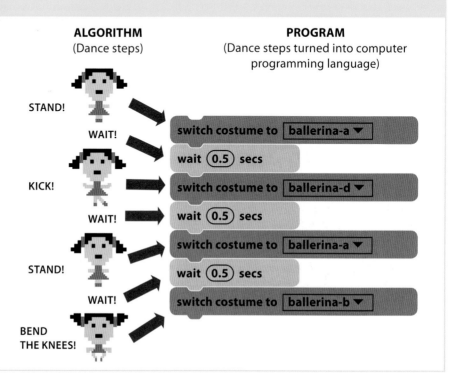

ALGORITHM
(Dance steps)

PROGRAM
(Dance steps turned into computer programming language)

STAND!

WAIT!

KICK!

WAIT!

STAND!

WAIT!

BEND THE KNEES!

```
switch costume to ballerina-a ▼
wait 0.5 secs
switch costume to ballerina-d ▼
wait 0.5 secs
switch costume to ballerina-a ▼
wait 0.5 secs
switch costume to ballerina-b ▼
```

30 Now for the second part of the ballerina's routine. After flexing her leg three times, she'll dip twice.

Costume ballerina-a then ballerina-b, repeated twice

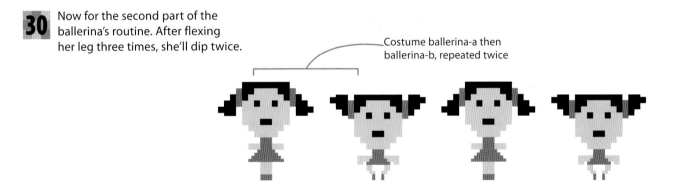

31 Add the blocks shown here to the bottom of the ballerina's script, after the first "repeat" block.

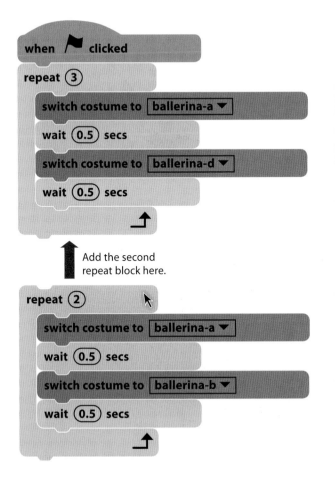

```
when 🏴 clicked
repeat (3)
    switch costume to [ballerina-a ▼]
    wait (0.5) secs
    switch costume to [ballerina-d ▼]
    wait (0.5) secs
    ↰
```

Add the second repeat block here.

```
repeat (2)
    switch costume to [ballerina-a ▼]
    wait (0.5) secs
    switch costume to [ballerina-b ▼]
    wait (0.5) secs
    ↰
```

32 Next, click the green flag and you'll see the ballerina do her full routine. But she'll only do the routine once. To make the dance go on we can wrap the whole body of the script in a "forever" loop. Loops inside loops!

Drag the "forever" loop to the top of the existing script and the jaws will expand to fit.

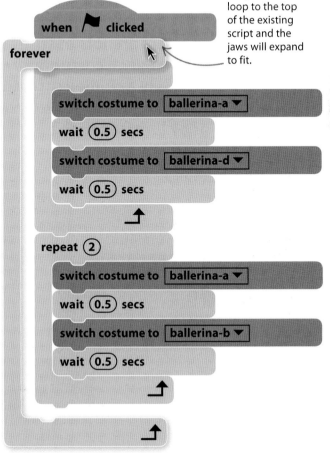

```
when 🏴 clicked
forever
    switch costume to [ballerina-a ▼]
    wait (0.5) secs
    switch costume to [ballerina-d ▼]
    wait (0.5) secs
    ↰
    repeat (2)
        switch costume to [ballerina-a ▼]
        wait (0.5) secs
        switch costume to [ballerina-b ▼]
        wait (0.5) secs
        ↰
    ↰
```

EXPERT TIPS

Repeat loops and forever loops

Look at the bottom of the two types of loop you've used so far. Which one can have blocks attached to it? You might spot that the "repeat" block has a small lug on the bottom, but the "forever" block doesn't. There's no lug on a "forever" loop because it goes on forever, so there's no point adding blocks after it. A "repeat" block, however, runs a fixed number of times and the script then continues.

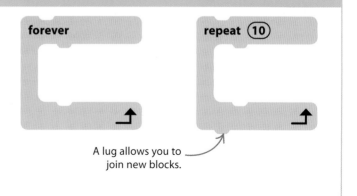

A lug allows you to join new blocks.

Hacks and tweaks

You can add as many dancers as you like to this project. There are lots of sprites in Scratch that have several costumes, and even those with only a single costume can be instructed to dance by flipping left to right or by jumping in the air.

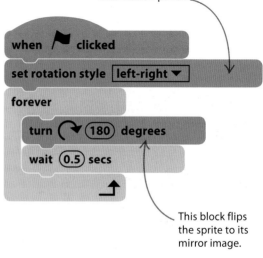

This is the same as selecting the double arrow rotation style in the sprite's information panel.

▽ **Turn around**
You can make any character face the other way by using a "turn 180 degrees" block. Just add this block before the end of the "forever" loop to make your sprite's dance switch direction each time.

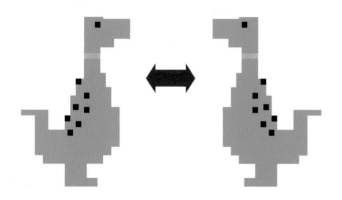

This block flips the sprite to its mirror image.

▷ Dance-off!

Look in the library for sprites with the word "Hip-Hop" in the name. They have lots of costumes showing different dance postures. Start off with a simple script like this one that shows all the costumes in order. Then choose the costumes that work best together and switch between them. Add loops to extend the dance or add sensing blocks to give you keyboard control.

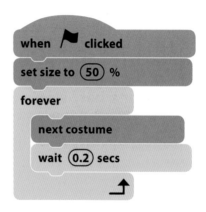

```
when 🏳 clicked
set size to (50) %
forever
    next costume
    wait (0.2) secs
```

▽ Might as well jump!

Add another ballerina and make her jump in the air with this script. The change of costume makes it seem like the ballerina is really jumping. Experiment with the timing to make the dance match the music.

```
when 🏳 clicked
set rotation style [left-right ▼]
forever
    switch costume to [ballerina-b ▼]
    wait (3) secs
    point in direction (0 ▼)
    move (50) steps
    switch costume to [ballerina-c ▼]
    wait (0.5) secs
    point in direction (180 ▼)
    move (50) steps
```

Choose 0 for upward movement.

Choose 180 for downward movement.

• • • TRY THIS

Shout!

Add this short script to every one of your sprites. When you press the x key, all the sprites will shout "Party!"

```
when [x ▼] key pressed
say [Party!] for (2) secs
```

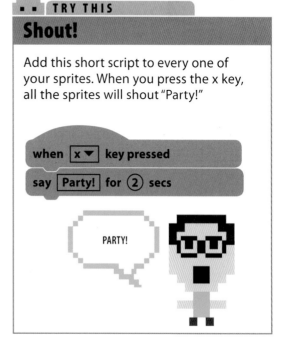

PARTY!

Animal Race

Have you ever wondered which is faster – a dog or a bat? Now you can find out when you play this fun fast-finger, button-pressing, two-player animal race game.

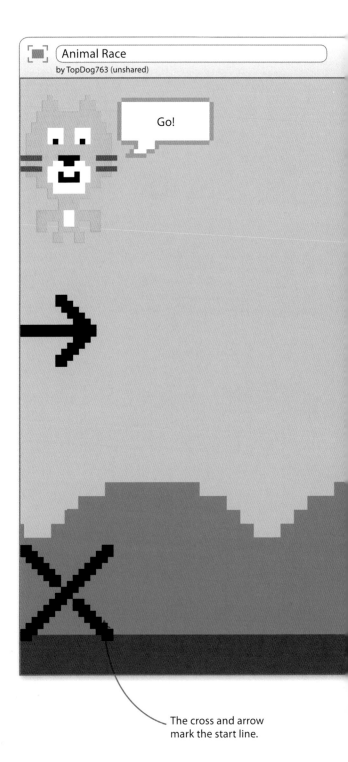

Animal Race
by TopDog763 (unshared)

Go!

How it works

The aim of this two-player game is simply to race across the screen and reach the balloons before the other player. Fast finger action is all you need to win. The faster you tap the keyboard's "z" or "m" key, the faster your sprite moves from left to right.

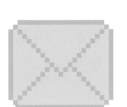

◁ **Sending messages**
This project shows you how to use Scratch's message feature to make one sprite pass information to other sprites, such as when the cat sprite tells the dog and bat to start racing.

◁ **Variables**
The cat's script stores information in something programmers call a variable. In this project, you'll use a variable to store the numbers for the cat's count at the start of the race.

Count

The cross and arrow mark the start line.

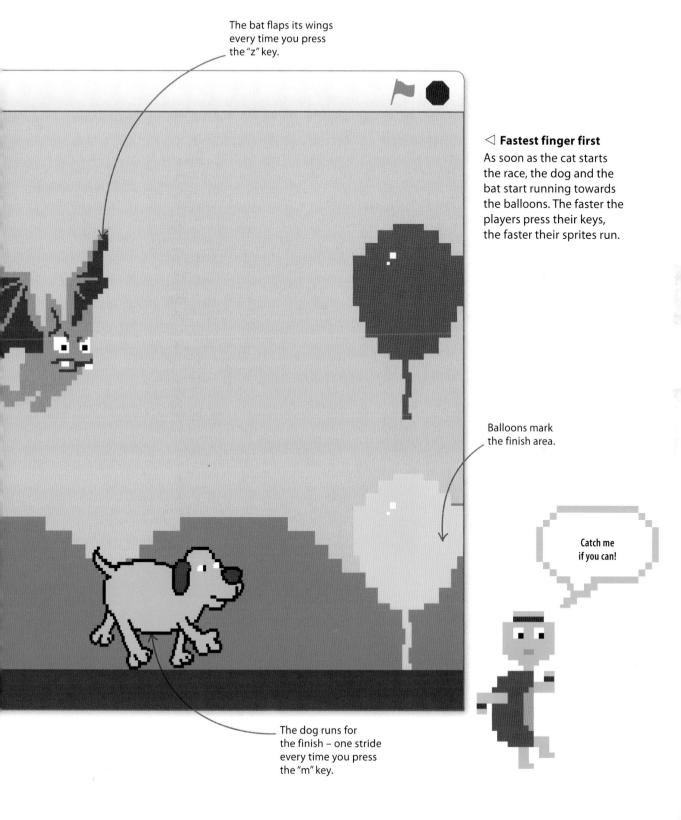

The bat flaps its wings every time you press the "z" key.

◁ **Fastest finger first**
As soon as the cat starts the race, the dog and the bat start running towards the balloons. The faster the players press their keys, the faster their sprites run.

Balloons mark the finish area.

Catch me if you can!

The dog runs for the finish – one stride every time you press the "m" key.

Starter cat

The cat starts the race with "1… 2… 3… Go!", so you need to teach him how to count. Computer programs use variables to store information that can change, such as a player's name or their score in a game. The cat will use a variable named "Count" to keep track of what number he's got up to.

1 Start a new project. To create a new variable, select the orange Data block in the blocks palette and click on the "Make a variable" button.

2 A small window will pop up asking you to give the new variable a name. Type "Count", leave everything else alone, and click the "OK" button.

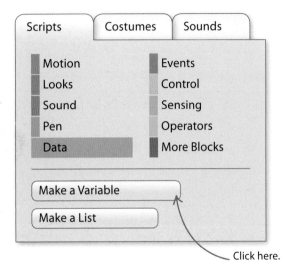

Click here.

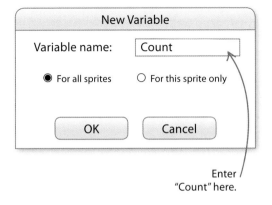

Enter "Count" here.

3 You'll now see some orange blocks for the new variable in the blocks palette. Uncheck the variable's tick box so that it doesn't appear on the stage.

Tick box

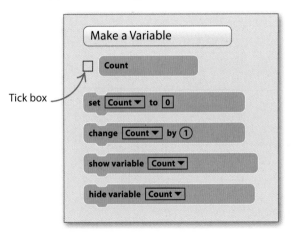

4 Make this script for the cat. It starts by setting the value of "Count" to zero. Next, inside a loop, it adds one to the value of "Count" and makes the cat say the new value for one second. The loop runs three times and then the cat says "Go!" to start the race.

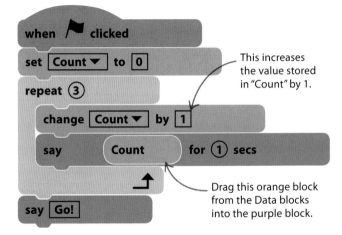

This increases the value stored in "Count" by 1.

Drag this orange block from the Data blocks into the purple block.

5 Click the green flag to run the script. The orange "Count" block in the window of the "say" block makes the cat say the variable's value each time. You can change how high the cat counts by changing the number in the "repeat" loop's window.

1... 2... 3

· · LINGO

Variables

Think of a variable as a box for storing information, with a label to remember what's inside. When you create a variable, give it a sensible name, such as "High Score" or "Player Name". You can put all sorts of data into variables, including numbers and words, and the data can change while the program is running.

95970

High Score

Setting up the racers

The cat is ready to start the race. The next steps are to decorate the stage for the race and then to add the bat and the dog sprites, along with other sprites to mark the start and end of the racetrack.

6 Add a backdrop. Click on the backdrop symbol 🖼 to the left of the sprites list and add the "blue sky" backdrop.

Stage
1 backdrop

New backdrop:

Click here to open the backdrop library.

7 It's time to add some sprites for the racers, starting with the dog. Click the sprite symbol 👤 in the sprites list. Find Dog2 in the library and add it to your project.

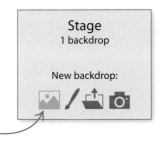

Sprites

Sprite1   Dog2

Dog2 will now appear in the sprites list.

8 Make sure Dog2 is selected in the sprites list. Click on the Costumes tab at the top of the blocks palette and you'll see it has three costumes. The first two show the dog running, but we don't need the third one so delete it.

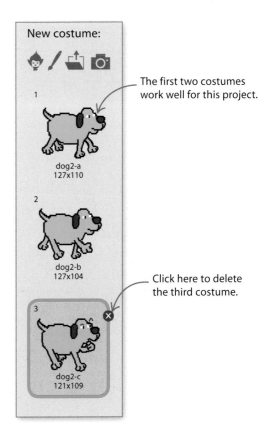

New costume:

1

dog2-a
127x110

The first two costumes work well for this project.

2

dog2-b
127x104

3

dog2-c
121x109

Click here to delete the third costume.

9 To tell the dog where to start the race, add another new sprite: Button5, which is a black cross. Drag it to the bottom left of the stage.

The black cross tells the dog where to start the race.

10 Every sprite you load should have a meaningful name. This makes scripts easier to understand. To rename Button5, click on the blue "i" and name it "Dog Start". Then click the blue triangle to return to the sprites list.

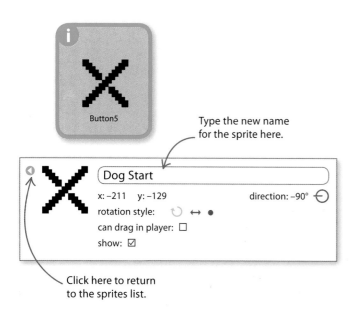

Type the new name for the sprite here.

Click here to return to the sprites list.

11 Select Dog2 again. Then click the Scripts tab at the top of the Scratch window and add this script to make the dog start in the correct place. Run the project to see it in action.

Choose "Dog Start" from the drop-down menu.

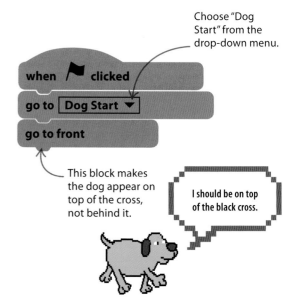

This block makes the dog appear on top of the cross, not behind it.

I should be on top of the black cross.

12 Now add a new sprite for the dog's finish line. Choose Balloon1, but rename it "Dog Finish". To change the balloon's colour, click on the Costumes tab and choose the yellow costume. On the stage, drag the sprite to the finish point of the dog's race.

Remember to choose the yellow balloon for the dog.

13 The dog needs someone to race against. Click the sprite symbol ✿ in the sprites list again and add Bat1 to the project. Click the Costumes tab and you'll see two costumes perfect for flapping.

14 Now add the Arrow2 sprite, but rename it "Bat Start" and drag it just above the cross. Then add another balloon, rename it "Bat Finish", and place it at the bat's finish line on the right.

The bat has to touch the balloon to finish the race.

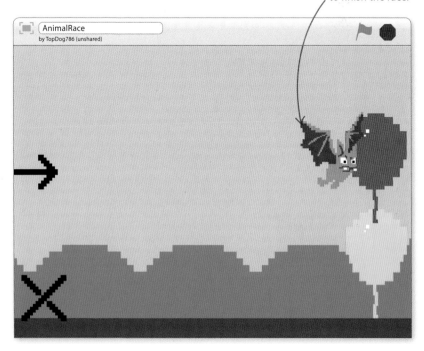

15 Select the bat sprite in the sprites list and give it this script. Run the project and watch the competitors line up at the start.

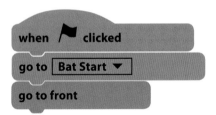

The race

The bat and the dog both need scripts to make them race. The cat will trigger these scripts by sending a message when it says "Go!" at the start of the race. Both contestants will receive the message at exactly the same time.

16 Select the cat sprite in the sprites list and add a "broadcast message1" block to the bottom of its script. This block sends out a message to every other sprite.

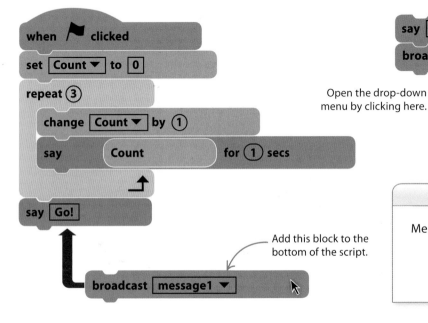

Add this block to the bottom of the script.

17 Click on the black triangle in the "broadcast" block and choose "new message" from the drop-down menu. Type "Start Race" as the name of the new message and click "OK".

Open the drop-down menu by clicking here.

18 Now the cat sends out the "Start Race" message at the start of the race. Each racer needs a script to make it react, so select the dog first and add this script. See how the two "wait until" blocks together make the player press the "m" key and then release it again and again to move their character; just keeping your finger on the "m" key won't work.

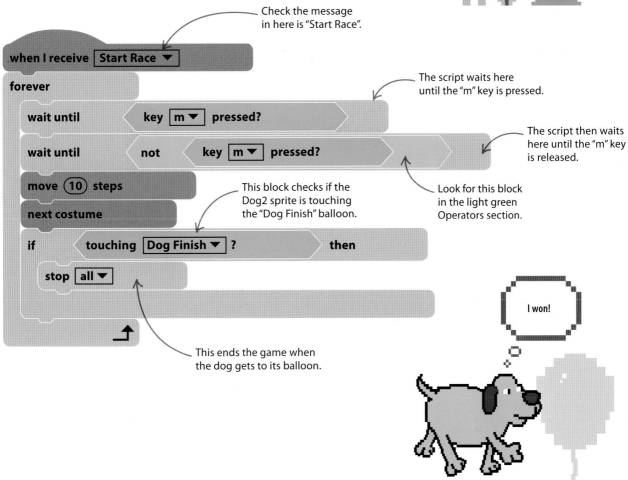

Check the message in here is "Start Race".

```
when I receive Start Race ▼
forever
    wait until          key  m ▼  pressed?
    wait until      not      key  m ▼  pressed?
    move 10 steps
    next costume
    if        touching Dog Finish ▼ ?        then
        stop all ▼
```

The script waits here until the "m" key is pressed.

The script then waits here until the "m" key is released.

This block checks if the Dog2 sprite is touching the "Dog Finish" balloon.

Look for this block in the light green Operators section.

This ends the game when the dog gets to its balloon.

I won!

. . . **LINGO**

Boolean operator: NOT

The "not" block reverses the answer to the question block inside it. This block is very useful for testing if something *isn't* happening. There are three green Operators blocks that can change answers to yes/no questions (or true/false statements) in useful ways: "not", "or", and "and". Programmers call these "Boolean operators" and you'll use all of them in this book.

19 Run the project. Once the cat says "Go!", you should find that the dog runs forward a step each time you press and release the "m" key. When it reaches its balloon, the dog should stop responding. If anything isn't working, carefully check your script against the version in the book.

20 Next, add this similar script to the bat sprite. The only differences are that the key selected now is the "z" key and the bat must touch its own finish sprite.

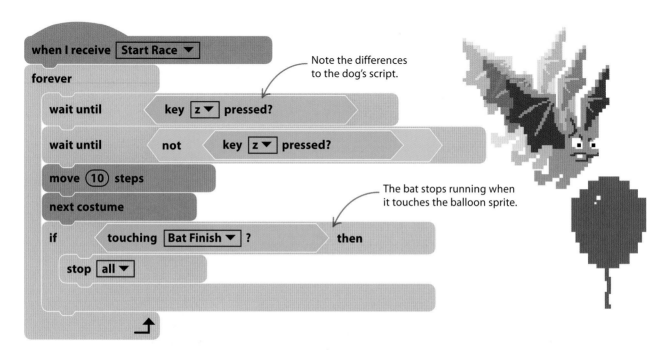

Note the differences to the dog's script.

The bat stops running when it touches the balloon sprite.

21 Now try to race the sprites. You might find that one sprite wins more easily because a wing or a nose sticks out. You can drag the start and finish sprites around a little to even things up.

Animal Race
by TopDog763 (unshared)

Go!

Drag the cat to the corner, out of the way of the racers.

Hacks and tweaks

The race game is very simple, but you can easily add features to make it more interesting. Here are some suggestions to get you started. It's worth making a copy of your project before you start to change things – then you won't be afraid to experiment.

▷ **Sounds**

Add a sound effect to mark the start of the race by adding a "play sound" block to the cat's script. The cat has the "meow" sound preloaded, but you can load other sounds from the sound library by clicking the Sounds tab and then the speaker symbol 🔊.

Click the drop-down menu to see the sounds loaded for this sprite.

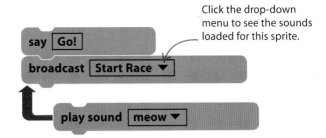

```
say Go!
broadcast Start Race ▼
        play sound meow ▼
```

Change 0 to 4.

```
set Count ▼ to 4
repeat 3
    change Count ▼ by (−1)
    say      Count        for 1 secs
```

Place a minus sign in front of 1.

◁ **Countdown**

Try changing the middle part of the cat's script to look like this. Can you work out what will happen now?

I'm the fastest!

◁ **Extra competitors**

Why not add more animals to the race? Find some sprites in the sprite library with costumes you can animate, like the parrots or Butterfly1. Add start and end sprites for each one of them and adapt the racing script to use different keys. If you need to adjust a sprite's size, just add a "set size" block.

▽ Challenging controls

You can make the game harder for the players by making them press two keys alternately rather than one key repeatedly. You just need to change the script to wait for a second key to be pressed and released after the first one. This shows how to change the dog's script. For the bat, make the same change but use "x" for the second key instead of "n".

FASTER, FASTER, KEEP GOING STRAIGHT!

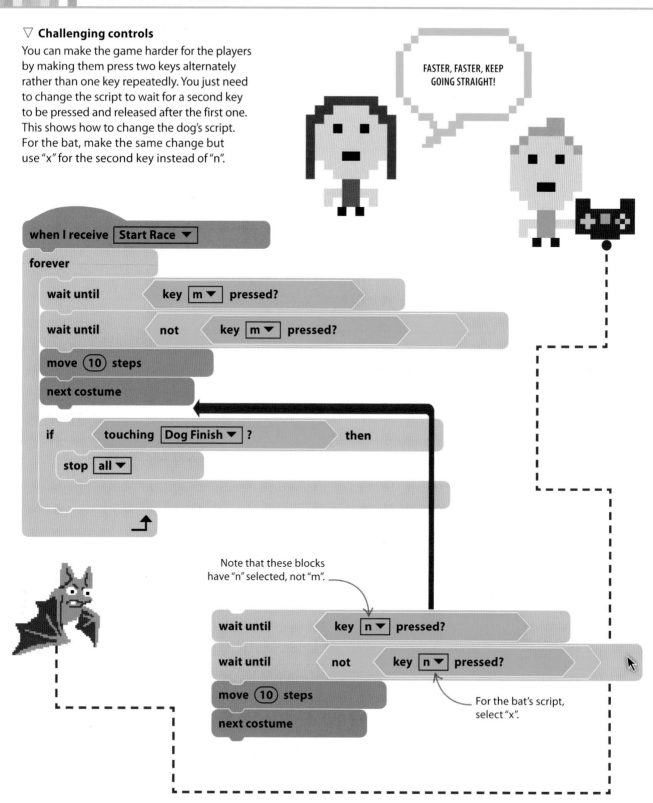

```
when I receive  Start Race ▼
forever
    wait until        key  m ▼  pressed?
    wait until   not      key  m ▼  pressed?
    move (10) steps
    next costume
    if         touching  Dog Finish ▼  ?        then
        stop  all ▼
```

Note that these blocks have "n" selected, not "m".

```
    wait until        key  n ▼  pressed?
    wait until   not      key  n ▼  pressed?
    move (10) steps
    next costume
```

For the bat's script, select "x".

Race positions

It might not always be easy to tell who's won if the finish is close. To fix this, you can make each animal show their finishing position when the game ends.

1 Choose Data in the blocks palette and then click the "Make a Variable" button to create a new variable. Call it "Position".

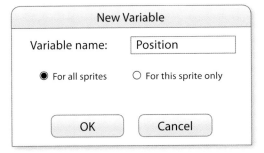

New Variable

Variable name: **Position**

● For all sprites   ○ For this sprite only

OK   Cancel

2 Next add a "set Position to" block to the bottom of the cat's script and change the number to one.

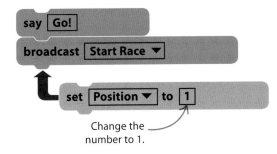

say [Go!]
broadcast [Start Race ▼]

set [Position ▼] to [1]

Change the number to 1.

3 Now change the end of the dog's script so it looks like this. You need to add two new blocks and choose a new menu option in the "stop" block. Do the same for the bat.

4 Try it out. The cat's script sets "Position" to 1. The first sprite to reach the finish runs the "think Position" block, which makes a thought bubble containing the number 1 appear. Their script then adds 1 to the value of "Position", making it 2. When the second sprite finishes and thinks of "Position", it displays 2.

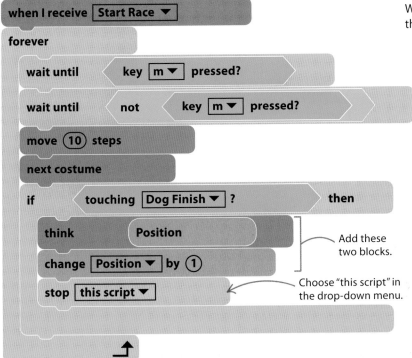

when I receive [Start Race ▼]

forever

wait until [key [m ▼] pressed?]

wait until [not [key [m ▼] pressed?]]

move (10) steps

next costume

if [touching [Dog Finish ▼] ?] then

think [Position]

change [Position ▼] by (1)

stop [this script ▼]

Add these two blocks.

Choose "this script" in the drop-down menu.

Ask Gobo

Do you have a tricky decision to make or want to predict the future? Let Gobo help you in this fortune-telling project. Here you'll learn about random numbers, variables, and how computer programs make choices.

How it works

Gobo invites you to ask a question and then answers with either "Yes" or "No". You can ask anything you like, from "Am I going to be a billionaire?" to "Should I play a computer game instead of doing my homework?" Gobo pauses to look like it's thinking, but its answers are actually pure chance.

◁ **Gobo**
Friendly Gobo is the only sprite in this project. It has three costumes that you can use later to help bring it to life.

◁ **Take a chance**
Just as the roll of the dice creates random numbers, Scratch can generate random numbers to make the program react in unpredictable ways.

Name of the project.

Ask Gobo
by FortuneTeller100 (unshared)

The green flag starts the project.

The red button stops the project.

◁ **Ask a question!**
Gobo works best if you ask it to make predictions or decisions for you. Don't ask factual questions as it'll often get the answer wrong!

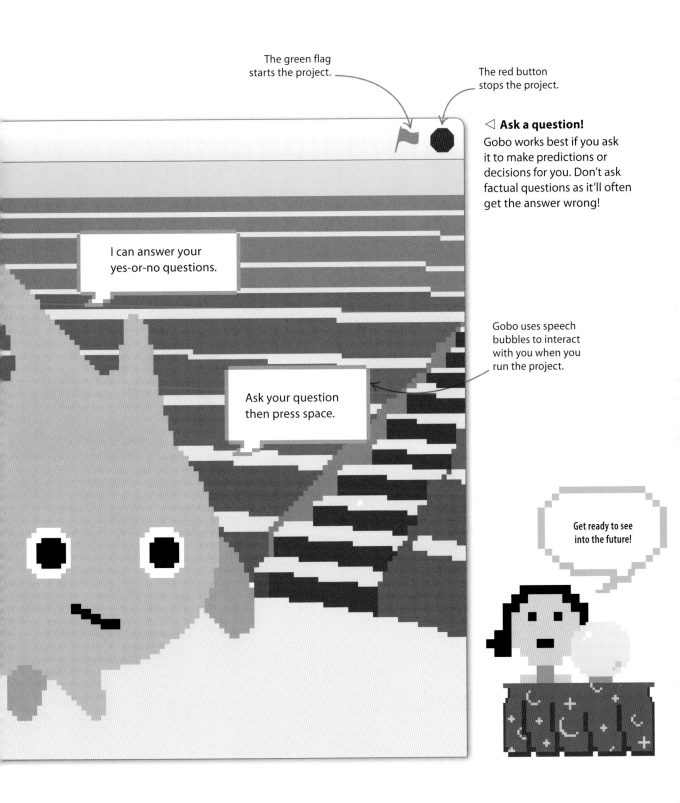

I can answer your yes-or-no questions.

Ask your question then press space.

Gobo uses speech bubbles to interact with you when you run the project.

Get ready to see into the future!

Setting the scene

Starting a project usually involves picking sprites and backdrops. Follow these steps to add the Gobo sprite to the project and to load a suitable backdrop to create a grand setting for Gobo's answers.

1 Start a new project. Then get rid of the cat sprite by right-clicking on it and selecting "delete".

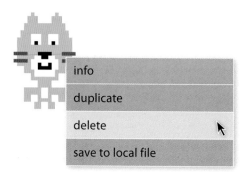

info

duplicate

delete

save to local file

2 To load the Gobo sprite, click on the sprite symbol ☻ in the sprites list. Choose Gobo and click "OK". Gobo will now appear in the sprites list.

Gobo

3 Gobo's a bit small, so add this script to make him bigger. Run the project and see him grow.

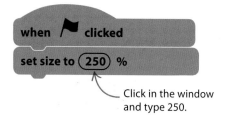

when 🏳 clicked

set size to (250) %

Click in the window and type 250.

4 Gobo's answers should be spoken in a serious setting. Click on the backdrop symbol 🖼 in the lower-left corner of the Scratch window and load the "greek theater" backdrop. Now drag Gobo to the centre with your mouse.

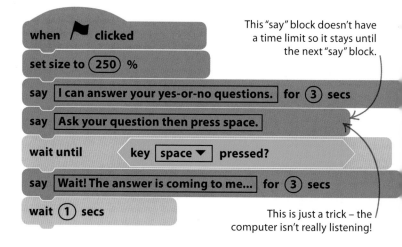

Ask Gobo
by FortuneTeller100 (unshared)

5 Select Gobo by clicking on it in the sprites list. Now add these extra blocks to your script to make it speak when the project starts. Run the new script and you'll see that it pauses until you press the space-bar. Gobo won't answer yet.

This "say" block doesn't have a time limit so it stays until the next "say" block.

when 🏳 clicked

set size to (250) %

say I can answer your yes-or-no questions. for (3) secs

say Ask your question then press space.

wait until < key space ▼ pressed? >

say Wait! The answer is coming to me... for (3) secs

wait (1) secs

This is just a trick – the computer isn't really listening!

Making random choices

Computers are usually very predictable. Often, with the same code and inputs, you'll get the same outputs, but you don't want that in this project. Gobo's script will mix things up with some random numbers.

6 You need to add some more blocks to create Gobo's answer. Gobo will reply in one of two ways, which we'll number one and two.

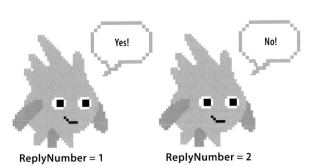

ReplyNumber = 1   ReplyNumber = 2

7 The script will use a variable named "ReplyNumber" to store the number of the reply the program has chosen so it can show the correct message. To make a new variable, choose the orange Data blocks at the top of the blocks palette. It won't have any blocks in it yet, so click the "Make a Variable" button.

8 A small window will pop up. Type "ReplyNumber" into the box to name the new variable and click "OK".

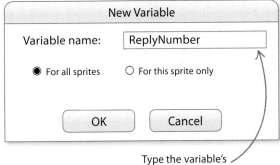

New Variable

Variable name: ReplyNumber

● For all sprites   ○ For this sprite only

OK   Cancel

Type the variable's name here.

9 You'll see that a block for your variable now appears in the Data blocks along with several other blocks.

If this tick box is ticked, the value of the variable is shown on the stage. Leave it ticked for now.

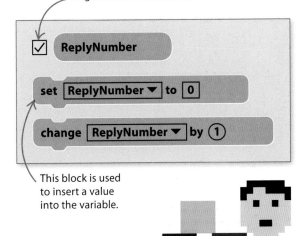

☑ ReplyNumber

set ReplyNumber ▼ to 0

change ReplyNumber ▼ by ①

This block is used to insert a value into the variable.

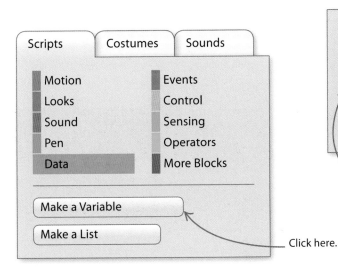

| Scripts | Costumes | Sounds |

Motion	Events
Looks	Control
Sound	Sensing
Pen	Operators
Data	More Blocks

Make a Variable

Make a List

Click here.

Random numbers

A random number is one that you can't predict before it appears. A dice roll is a random number – any of the numbers from one to six could appear each time you roll the dice. You don't know which number will come up until you roll. In Scratch, you can get a random number using the "pick random" block. Drag this block into the scripts area and experiment with it.

Lowest number it can select

If you click on the block it will tell you its value. It selects a random number each time.

pick random ① to ⑥

Highest number it can select

---

10 The variable will hold the number of Gobo's reply, but the program needs a way to choose that number randomly. Add a "set ReplyNumber to" block to the bottom of Gobo's script and then drag a green "pick random" block into it from the Operators section. Change the second number to two. The green block picks randomly between one and two, like flipping a coin.

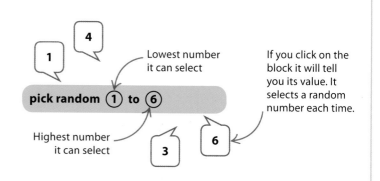

set ReplyNumber ▼ to ☐

pick random ① to ②

Change the second number to 2.

---

11 Next create this block to add to the bottom of the script. It will make Gobo say "Yes!" if the value in the variable "ReplyNumber" is one. The "say" block only runs if the value is one, otherwise it's skipped.

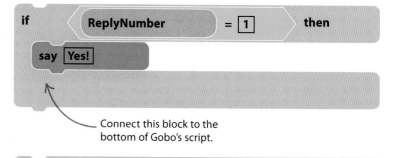

if ⟨ ReplyNumber = 1 ⟩ then

say Yes!

Connect this block to the bottom of Gobo's script.

---

12 Now run the project a few times. Around half the time Gobo will say "Yes!" The other times it doesn't say anything. If you look at the top of the stage, you'll see the "ReplyNumber" variable says one when you get "Yes!" and two when you get no reply. Add this extra block to make Gobo say "No!" when the variable is two.

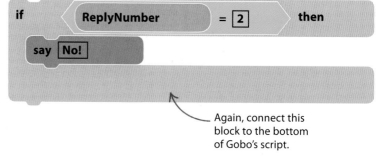

if ⟨ ReplyNumber = 2 ⟩ then

say No!

Again, connect this block to the bottom of Gobo's script.

13 The script should now look like this. Run the project a few times and check that Gobo gives random "yes" and "no" answers. If not, check the whole script carefully.

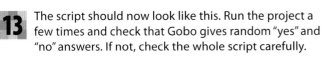

Wait! The answer is coming to me...

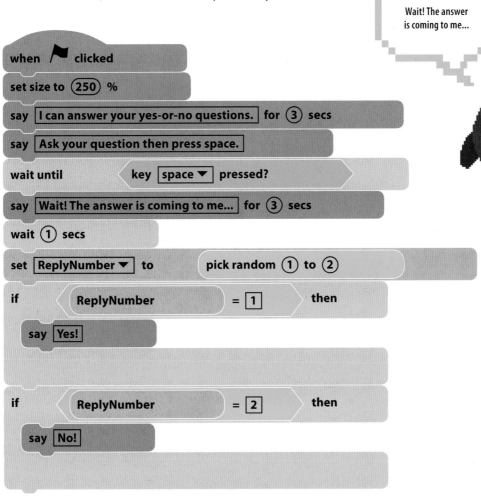

```
when ⚑ clicked
set size to (250) %
say [ I can answer your yes-or-no questions. ] for (3) secs
say [ Ask your question then press space. ]
wait until < key [ space ▼ ] pressed? >
say [ Wait! The answer is coming to me... ] for (3) secs
wait (1) secs
set [ ReplyNumber ▼ ] to ( pick random (1) to (2) )
if < ReplyNumber = [1] > then
    say [ Yes! ]

if < ReplyNumber = [2] > then
    say [ No! ]
```

14 You can now go to the Data blocks section and untick the "ReplyNumber" block to remove the variable from the stage.

If you use the offline version of Scratch, don't forget to save your work from time to time.

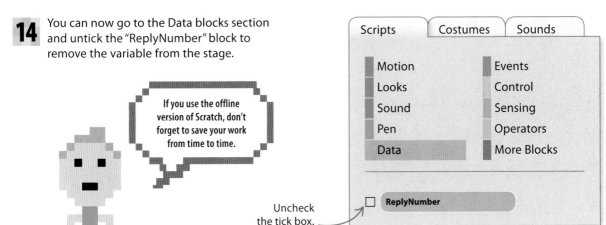

Scripts	Costumes	Sounds

Motion   Events
Looks   Control
Sound   Sensing
Pen   Operators
Data   More Blocks

☐ ReplyNumber

Uncheck the tick box.

15 Now try using your project to answer some important questions to predict the future!

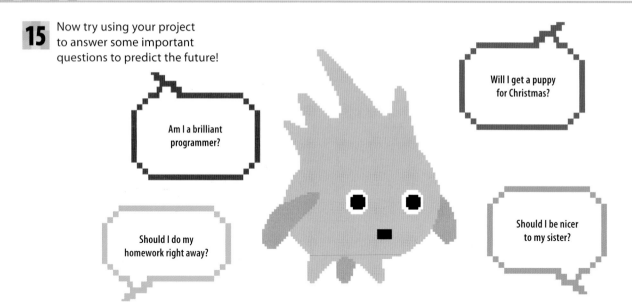

Will I get a puppy for Christmas?

Am I a brilliant programmer?

Should I do my homework right away?

Should I be nicer to my sister?

More decisions

You've already seen how to use "if then" blocks containing questions to decide whether or not to run lines of code. In this project, you use green Operators blocks inside "if then" blocks to check the value of a variable. The pale blue question blocks have "yes" or "no" answers, but when you use the green blocks you should ask if what they say is true or false.

There are three different green blocks you can use to compare numbers, each with a different job and symbol: = (equal to), > (greater than), and < (less than). Programmers call true-or-false decisions used inside "if then" blocks "Boolean conditions". They are named after the English mathematician George Boole (1815–1864).

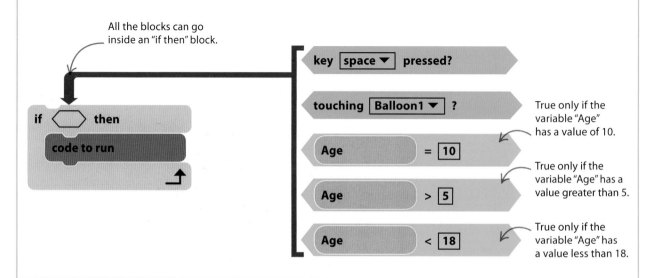

All the blocks can go inside an "if then" block.

if ⬡ then
code to run

key space ▼ pressed?

touching Balloon1 ▼ ?

Age = 10

True only if the variable "Age" has a value of 10.

Age > 5

True only if the variable "Age" has a value greater than 5.

Age < 18

True only if the variable "Age" has a value less than 18.

Hacks and tweaks

You can do much more with the random numbers than simply answering yes-or-no questions. Try exploring some of these possibilities.

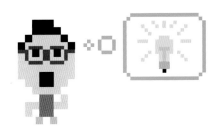

▽ **Ask me another**

To make Gobo answer more questions after the first one, place the original script inside a "forever" loop, as shown here, with a few extra blocks to make Gobo prompt the user for a new question.

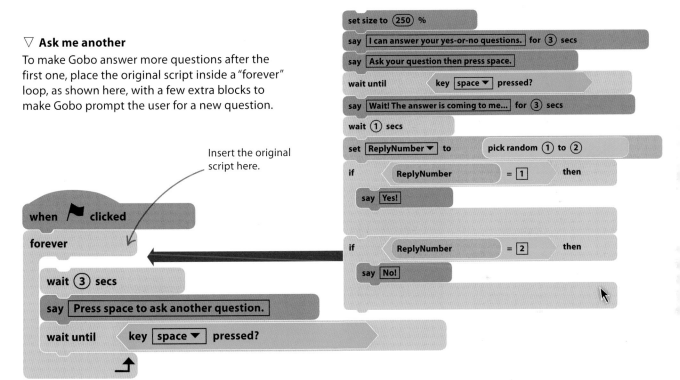

Insert the original script here.

```
when 🏳 clicked

forever
    wait 3 secs
    say Press space to ask another question.
    wait until    key space ▼ pressed?
```

```
set size to 250 %
say I can answer your yes-or-no questions. for 3 secs
say Ask your question then press space.
wait until    key space ▼ pressed?
say Wait! The answer is coming to me... for 3 secs
wait 1 secs
set ReplyNumber ▼ to    pick random 1 to 2
if    ReplyNumber = 1    then
    say Yes!

if    ReplyNumber = 2    then
    say No!
```

▷ **Special effects**

You can alter Gobo's replies to be more fun. While you're at it, why not make Gobo change colour or costume for each reply? You could also add sounds to its replies, some dance steps, or a spin.

How DARE you ask that!

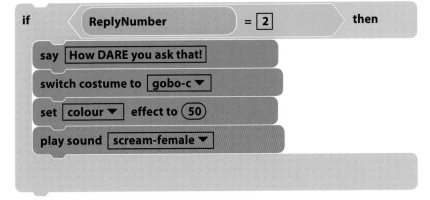

```
if    ReplyNumber = 2    then
    say How DARE you ask that!
    switch costume to gobo-c ▼
    set colour ▼ effect to 50
    play sound scream-female ▼
```

▽ More replies

To add to the fun you can extend the number of replies. You simply need to increase the top number in the "pick random" block to the new number of choices and then add extra "if then" blocks containing new "say" blocks. This example has six possible answers, but you can add as many as you like.

Change the 2 into a 6. This must match your number of replies or some responses will never appear.

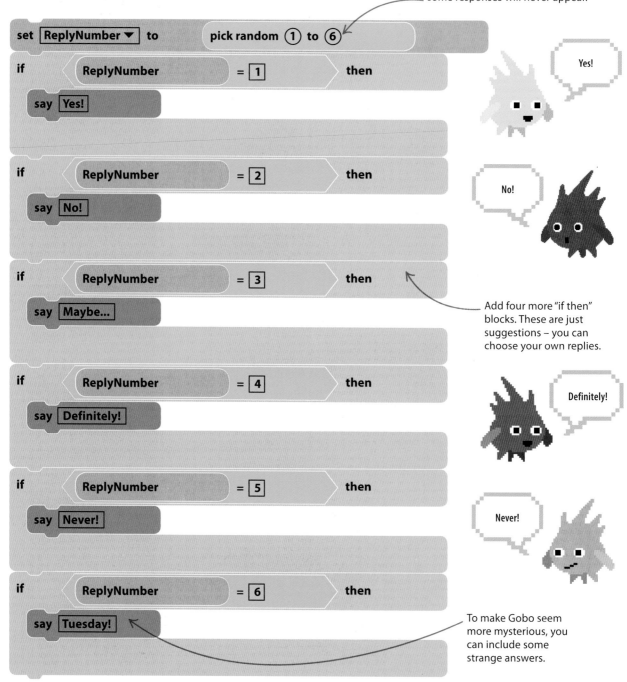

set ReplyNumber ▼ to　pick random ① to ⑥

if　ReplyNumber = 1　then
　say Yes!

if　ReplyNumber = 2　then
　say No!

if　ReplyNumber = 3　then
　say Maybe...

Add four more "if then" blocks. These are just suggestions – you can choose your own replies.

if　ReplyNumber = 4　then
　say Definitely!

if　ReplyNumber = 5　then
　say Never!

if　ReplyNumber = 6　then
　say Tuesday!

To make Gobo seem more mysterious, you can include some strange answers.

Yes!

No!

Definitely!

Never!

▽ Counting horse

You don't have to stick to yes-or-no answers – instead, you could answer questions like "How old am I?" or "What's my IQ?" with random numbers. Start a new project, load the Horse1 sprite, and add the script below to make it count out the answers by stomping up and down with its feet. You could also add some horse noises from the sound library.

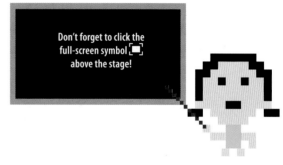

Don't forget to click the full-screen symbol above the stage!

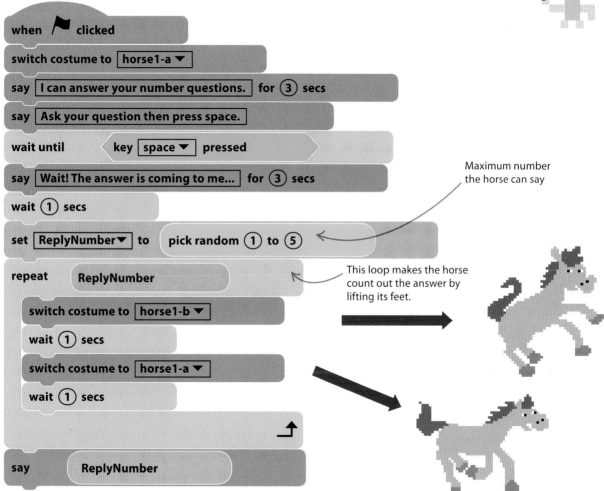

```
when ⚑ clicked
switch costume to horse1-a ▼
say I can answer your number questions. for 3 secs
say Ask your question then press space.
wait until   key space ▼ pressed
say Wait! The answer is coming to me... for 3 secs
wait 1 secs
set ReplyNumber ▼ to   pick random 1 to 5
repeat   ReplyNumber
    switch costume to horse1-b ▼
    wait 1 secs
    switch costume to horse1-a ▼
    wait 1 secs
say   ReplyNumber
```

Maximum number the horse can say

This loop makes the horse count out the answer by lifting its feet.

▷ Do as I say!

Rather than answering questions, Gobo could give random orders, such as "run up and down the stairs", "jump in the air twice", or "sing a famous song". Just change the text in the "say" blocks to Gobo's commands. You could also change Gobo's appearance to something grumpy to match the mood.

Take a hike!

Funny Faces

You can have lots of fun drawing your own sprites in Scratch – you don't have to stick to the ones in the sprite library. Creating your own sprites will give your projects a unique look. For this project, you can go wild making facial features and accessories for a DIY face.

How it works

This project starts with a blank face surrounded by a collection of eyes, noses, and other items that you can drag into the middle to create crazy expressions. Press the green flag to reset the face and start again.

You can add up to 11 eyes, but most sprites are just a single item.

Funny Faces
by MonsterFace321 (unshared)

Empty face

Bow tie

Mouth

Go ahead and create
as many funny faces
as you like!

△ **Funny, funnier, funniest!**
This project lets you use your creativity and
imagination to the fullest. You don't have
to make human faces. You can make aliens,
monsters, or anything!

Type in the name of
your project here.

Funny Faces

by MonsterFace321 (unshared)

Pig nose

Snotty
nose

Tongue

Get painting

Dust off your digital overalls because it's time for some painting. Scratch has a great paint editor built in, so you have all the tools you need to create a mini-masterpiece for each body part and item of clothing.

1 Start a new project and remove the cat sprite by right-clicking on it in the sprites list and selecting "delete". You're going to make your own sprites, so click on the paint symbol / above the sprites list to create the first one.

Click here to open the paint editor.

2 Scratch's paint editor will now open. You can use the paint editor to draw your own sprites. Make sure "Bitmap Mode" is selected in the bottom right.

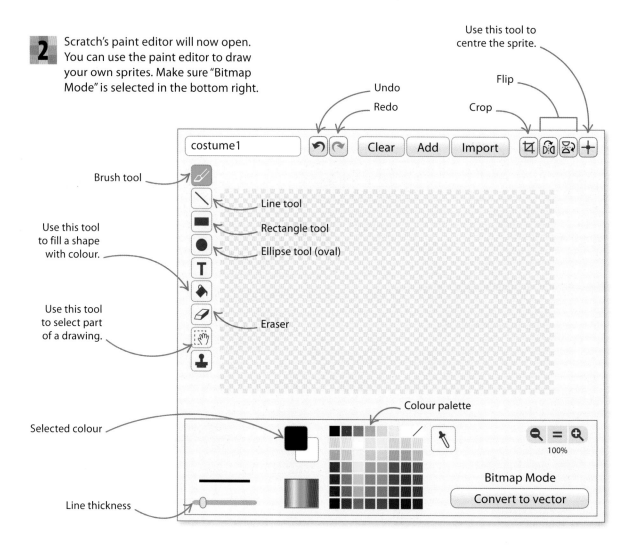

Use this tool to centre the sprite.

Flip

Undo

Redo

Crop

Brush tool

Line tool

Use this tool to fill a shape with colour.

Rectangle tool

Ellipse tool (oval)

Use this tool to select part of a drawing.

Eraser

Colour palette

Selected colour

Line thickness

3 Click on the brush tool in the upper left corner of the paint editor. Then click and draw an oval shape to form the head for your funny face. The middle should be near the small cross in the centre of the painting area.

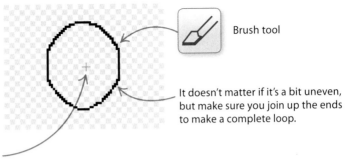

Brush tool

It doesn't matter if it's a bit uneven, but make sure you join up the ends to make a complete loop.

Centre the shape on the small cross.

4 Now choose the fill tool, which looks like a bucket of paint being tipped over. Click in the colour palette at the bottom to choose a colour for the face. Then click inside the head to fill it with your chosen colour.

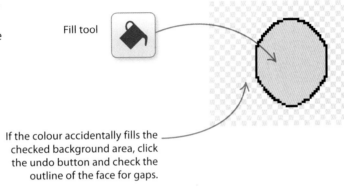

Fill tool

If the colour accidentally fills the checked background area, click the undo button and check the outline of the face for gaps.

5 Now check where Scratch thinks the centre of the head is by clicking the centre tool in the top right. A cross will appear on the paint editor – this shows the sprite's centre. You can click to move it.

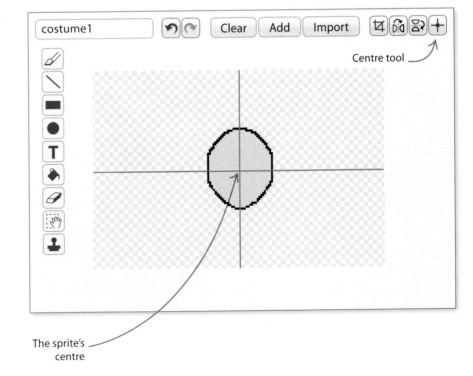

costume1   Clear   Add   Import

Centre tool

The sprite's centre

6 Well done – you've created a head! As a finishing touch, click the blue "i" symbol on this sprite in the sprites list and change the name to "Head" in the information panel.

Change name here.

7 The head needs to be in the centre of the stage when the Funny Face project runs. The project will position every sprite on the screen at the start to keep things tidy. To do this for the head, add this script.

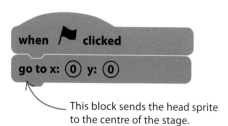

This block sends the head sprite to the centre of the stage.

EXPERT TIPS
Coordinates

To pinpoint any spot on the stage you can use two numbers called coordinates. The x coordinate, written first, tells you how far the point is across the stage horizontally. The y coordinate, written second, tells you how far the point is up or down the stage vertically. The x coordinates go from −240 to 240. The y coordinates go from −180 to 180. The coordinates of a point are written as (x, y). The centre of the bow tie on the right, for instance, has coordinates (215, 90).

Every spot on the stage has a unique pair of coordinates that can be used to position a sprite exactly.

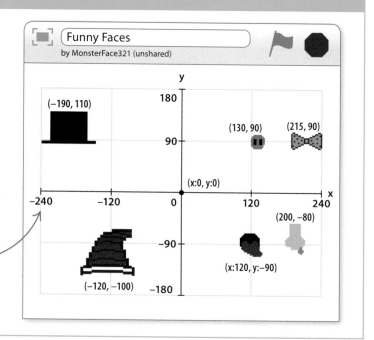

Time to make lots of sprites

The more different eyes, noses, mouths, ears, hats, and accessories your Funny Face project has, the more silly faces you can make, so spend some time making as many as you can. It's great fun. You can also find useful items in Scratch's costumes library, such as hats and sunglasses. You can skip the drawing stages for those.

8 Follow steps 8–13 to create your own items. Click on the paint symbol ✏ in the sprites list to create the new sprite. Use the paint editor tools to draw it, following the tips shown on this page.

Click the icon to create a new sprite.

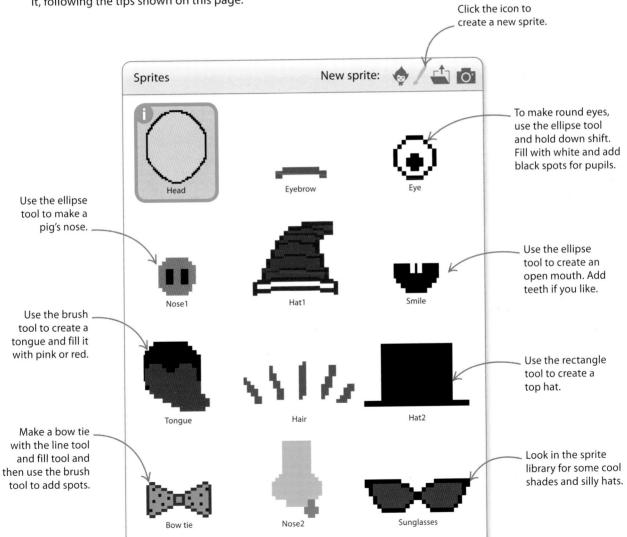

To make round eyes, use the ellipse tool and hold down shift. Fill with white and add black spots for pupils.

Use the ellipse tool to make a pig's nose.

Use the ellipse tool to create an open mouth. Add teeth if you like.

Use the brush tool to create a tongue and fill it with pink or red.

Use the rectangle tool to create a top hat.

Make a bow tie with the line tool and fill tool and then use the brush tool to add spots.

Look in the sprite library for some cool shades and silly hats.

Sprites   New sprite:

Head   Eyebrow   Eye

Nose1   Hat1   Smile

Tongue   Hair   Hat2

Bow tie   Nose2   Sunglasses

9 Remember to set the middle of each sprite with the centre tool.

Centre tool

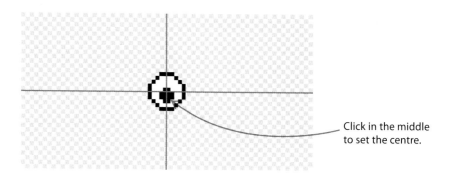

Click in the middle to set the centre.

10 Click the blue "i" on each sprite in the sprites list and give your creation a meaningful name. Also make sure the "can drag in player" check box is ticked so you can drag the sprite around the stage in full-screen mode.

Type a name for the sprite here.

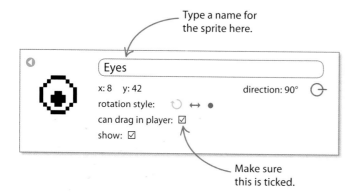

Make sure this is ticked.

11 When you've finished drawing a sprite, drag it across the stage to its starting position outside the face. Don't worry if the sprites overlap a bit.

12 To make the new sprite appear in the right place when you run the project, use the mouse to drag it to its start position and then give it a script like this one. The "go to" block in the blocks palette will automatically show the sprite's current coordinates.

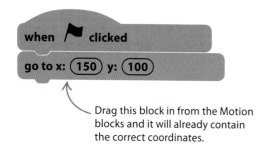

Drag this block in from the Motion blocks and it will already contain the correct coordinates.

13 Go back to step 8 and repeat the process until you have all the sprites you want.

Hey, this is a loop!

14 Now add a plain backdrop. Look in the stage info area to the left of the sprites list and you'll see a row of small symbols. Click the paint symbol / to paint a new backdrop. Then choose a colour from the palette and use the fill tool to fill the whole of the white area.

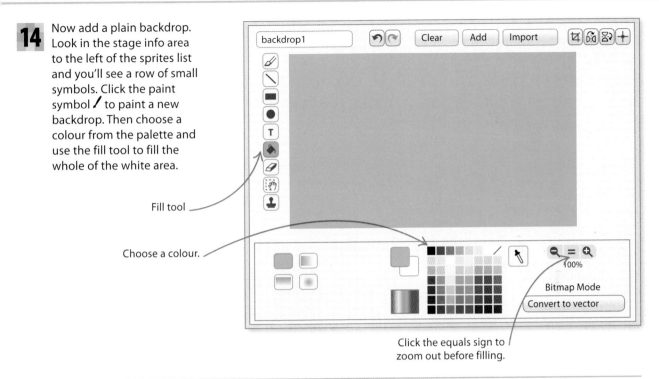

Fill tool

Choose a colour.

Click the equals sign to zoom out before filling.

Clones

You might want to use some sprites lots of times – perhaps your face will be funnier with ten eyes rather than two. Scratch allows you to "clone" a sprite to make fully working copies.

15 Make ten clones of the eye sprite by adding this loop to its script. Now when you run the project you can place all 11 eyes!

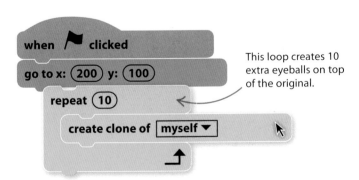

when ⚑ clicked

go to x: (200) y: (100)

repeat (10)

create clone of [myself ▼]

This loop creates 10 extra eyeballs on top of the original.

EXPERT TIPS

Clones

Clones work a bit like the "stamp" block you used in the Cat Art project. But while "stamp" just draws a picture on the backdrop, the clone block creates a working sprite. Clones can be used for lots of clever things, as you'll see in later projects.

create clone of [myself ▼]

This block makes an identical copy of a sprite in exactly the same position on the stage.

Hacks and tweaks

Funny Faces is great fun to extend. Create more silly
sprites and think about how to make them move.
As a finishing touch, you can frame your creation!

▽ Special effects

Can't see the eyes through the glasses? No
problem – make the sunglasses transparent
with Scratch's ghost effect. You'll find the block
in the Looks section, where it's called "set colour
effect". Change "colour" to "ghost" in its menu.

Increase the number
to make the sunglasses
more transparent.

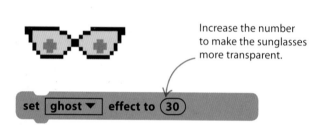

`set ghost ▼ effect to (30)`

▽ Spinning tie

Bring your sprites to life by making them
move. To make the bow tie spin around,
add a "forever" loop containing a "turn" block.

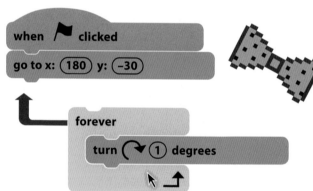

`when ⚑ clicked`
`go to x: (180) y: (-30)`

`forever`
`    turn ↻ (1) degrees`

▽ Snotty nose

To make disgusting green snot drip out of
the nose, create two new costumes for the
nose with spots of green colour. Then add
these new blocks to make the snot drip.

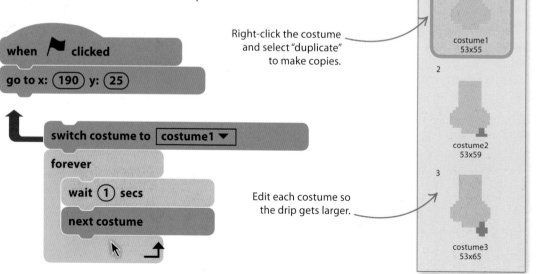

`when ⚑ clicked`
`go to x: (190) y: (25)`

`switch costume to costume1 ▼`
`forever`
`    wait (1) secs`
`    next costume`

Right-click the costume
and select "duplicate"
to make copies.

costume1
53x55

costume2
53x59

Edit each costume so
the drip gets larger.

costume3
53x65

In the frame

To create a neat frame around your funny face, follow these steps.

1 Click the paint symbol / in the sprites list to create a new sprite in the paint editor. Before you start painting, open the Scripts tab and give the sprite these scripts. They hide the frame at the start and make it appear when you press the space-bar and disappear when you press the "c" key.

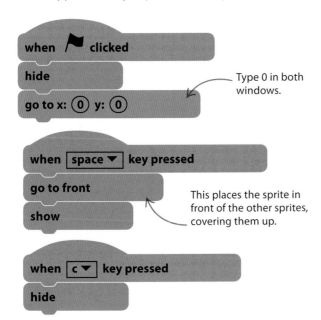

when ⚑ clicked
hide
go to x: ⓪ y: ⓪

Type 0 in both windows.

when space ▼ key pressed
go to front
show

This places the sprite in front of the other sprites, covering them up.

when c ▼ key pressed
hide

2 Run the project to centre the sprite. Next click the Costumes tab to return to the paint editor. Choose black in the colour palette and use the fill tool to fill the white area with black. Then use the select tool to draw a rectangle in the middle, and press "delete" on your keyboard to make a hole. Check the stage to see if the frame is the right shape and adjust as needed.

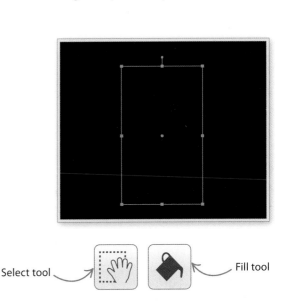

Select tool ⟶ ⬚✋   🖌 ⟵ Fill tool

3 Now run the project. Make a silly face and then check if you can make the frame appear and disappear with the space-bar and "c" key.

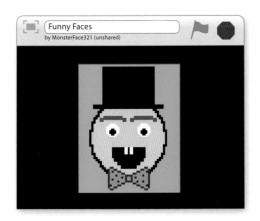

Funny Faces
by MonsterFace321 (unshared)

TRY THIS
Try something different

You can use this project to create anything from snowmen and Christmas trees to monsters and aliens!

Art

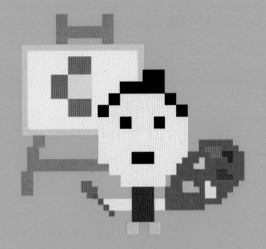

Birthday Card

Who wants an ordinary birthday card when you can have an animated feast for the eyes and ears? Scratch is the perfect tool for making a birthday card. This card has singing sharks, but you can adapt the project to make someone their own unique card.

How it works

When you run this project, a mysterious flashing green button appears. Press the button and an animated birthday card fills the screen, complete with singing sharks. The sharks take turns singing the lines of the "Happy Birthday" song.

Be sure to run this project in full-screen mode.

The sharks drop in from the top and then sing "Happy Birthday".

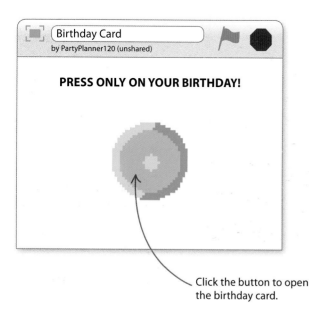

Click the button to open the birthday card.

A balloon-filled backdrop sets the scene.

The animated sign at the top rocks from side to side.

BIRTHDAY!

The cake slides into view from the edge of the stage.

△ **Gliding around**
This project uses the "glide" block, which makes sprites move smoothly around the stage. You need to use Scratch's coordinates system to set the exact start and finish point of each glide. If you can't remember how coordinates work, see the Funny Faces project.

△ **Keeping time**
Like Animal Race, this project uses messages sent from one sprite to another to control the timing of scripts. The singing sharks send messages back and forth to time their lines of "Happy Birthday".

Birthday button

To avoid spoiling the surprise of the card, all that appears when the project is run is a message and a button for the birthday person to press.

Surprise!

1 Start a new project. Remove the cat sprite by right-clicking on it in the sprites list and selecting "delete". Load the Button1 sprite from the sprite library.

Button1

2 Add these two scripts to Button1. The first one makes the button appear in the centre of the stage and flash invitingly when the project starts. The second one runs after the button is clicked, making the button disappear and sending a message to launch the rest of the card. After adding the "broadcast" block, open its pop-up menu, choose "new message", and call the message "Go!"

This block positions the button in the centre of the stage.

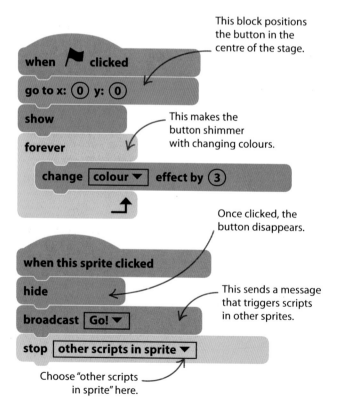

This makes the button shimmer with changing colours.

Once clicked, the button disappears.

This sends a message that triggers scripts in other sprites.

Choose "other scripts in sprite" here.

3 To add the sign saying "PRESS ONLY ON YOUR BIRTHDAY!", you need to edit the backdrop. First select the stage by clicking the small white rectangle to the left of the sprites list. Then click the Backdrops tab above the blocks palette.

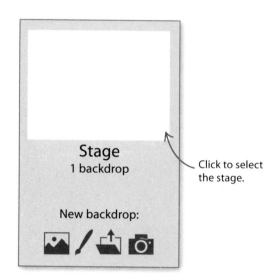

Stage
1 backdrop

Click to select the stage.

New backdrop:

Click this tab to edit the backdrop.

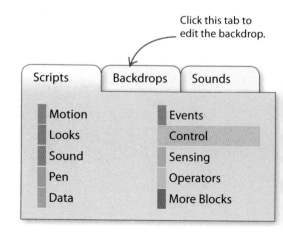

Scripts	Backdrops	Sounds
Motion		Events
Looks		Control
Sound		Sensing
Pen		Operators
Data		More Blocks

4 Scratch's paint editor will now open. Choose the text tool **T** and click in the large white area, about a third of the way down. Type the words "PRESS ONLY ON YOUR BIRTHDAY!" If you want to re-type the message for any reason, use the select tool to draw a box around the text and press delete on your keyboard before starting again.

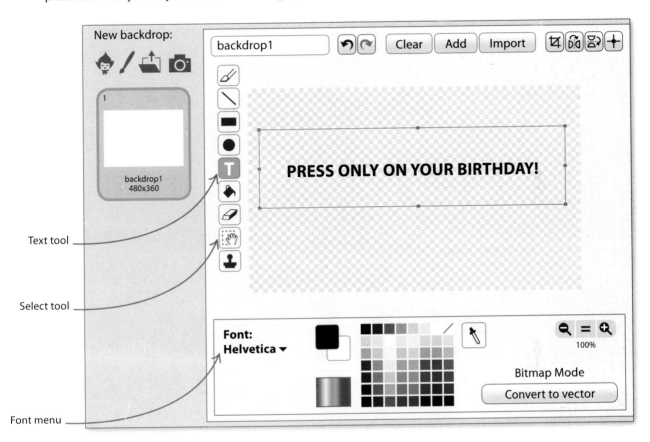

Text tool

Select tool

Font menu

5 You can choose a font using the font menu at the bottom left of the paint editor. "Mystery" works well for a birthday card.

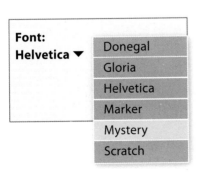

6 Use the select tool to resize or move the text until you're happy with it.

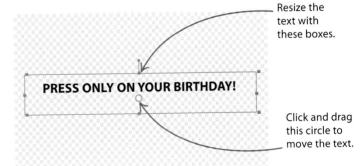

Resize the text with these boxes.

Click and drag this circle to move the text.

7 For the card itself you need a different backdrop. Click the backdrop symbol in the lower left of the Scratch window to choose a new backdrop from the library. Then select the "party" backdrop.

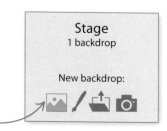

Click here to open the backdrops library.

8 Make sure you still have the stage selected in the lower left of the Scratch window and not one of the sprites. Click on the Scripts tab above the blocks palette and add these scripts for the stage. Now try running the project and see what happens when you click the button.

This block shows the white backdrop.

The "party" backdrop with balloons appears when the button is pressed.

Enter the cake

Once the button is pressed, the card opens. The button's script broadcasts the "Go!" message to all the sprites to trigger the animations and music.

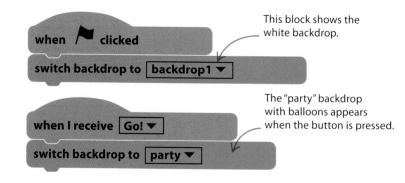

9 What else does a birthday need besides a card? A cake! Click on the sprite symbol ♠ in the sprites list and add the Cake sprite to the project.

10 Before you create the cake's scripts, you need to load the birthday song. Click the Sounds tab at the top of the Scratch window and then the speaker icon 🔊 to choose a sound from the library. Select the sound called "birthday" and click "OK".

Click here first.

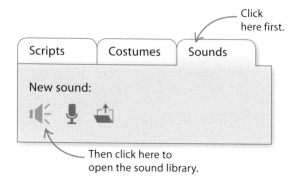

Then click here to open the sound library.

11 We want the cake to slide in from the left, starting from a position off-stage. If we send the cake to the edge of the stage (−240, −100), half of it will show because that's the position of the cake's centre. You can't send a sprite completely off the screen, so we'll send it to (−300, −100), so that only a tiny bit shows.

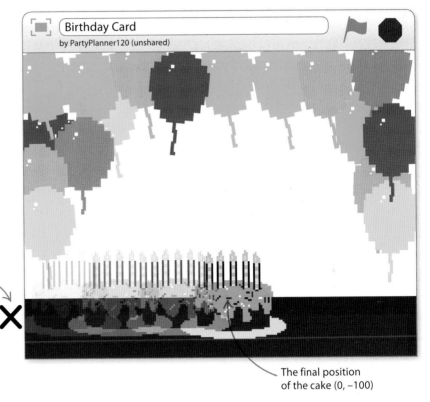

Birthday Card
by PartyPlanner120 (unshared)

The starting position of the cake (−300, −100)

The final position of the cake (0, −100)

12 Add these scripts to the cake to hide it when the project runs, and then make it glide in from the left when the green button is pressed. Note that the cake broadcasts a new message, called "Line1". Later you'll use this to make one of the sharks sing the first line of "Happy Birthday".

This is the cake's starting position off the left of the stage.

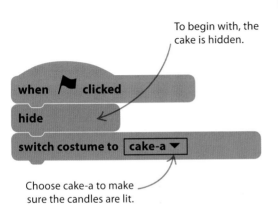

To begin with, the cake is hidden.

when 🏴 clicked
hide
switch costume to [cake-a ▼]

Choose cake-a to make sure the candles are lit.

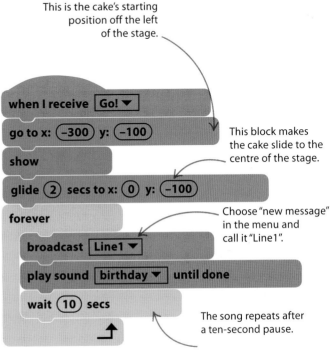

when I receive [Go! ▼]
go to x: (−300) y: (−100)
show
glide (2) secs to x: (0) y: (−100)
forever
    broadcast [Line1 ▼]
    play sound [birthday ▼] until done
    wait (10) secs

This block makes the cake slide to the centre of the stage.

Choose "new message" in the menu and call it "Line1".

The song repeats after a ten-second pause.

Birthday banner

The next thing needed for a party atmosphere is an animated birthday banner that rocks back and forth.

13 The banner will be a sprite, but this time you'll create a new sprite by painting it rather than loading it from the library. Click the paint symbol ✏ in the sprites list and the paint editor will open. A new sprite will appear in the sprites list. Click the blue "i" symbol on the sprite and rename the sprite "Banner".

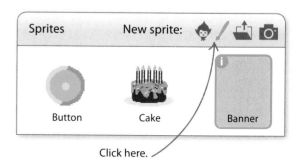

Click here.

14 Draw your birthday banner in the paint editor. Use the rectangle tool to create the banner, either as a solid colour or just an outline. Then use the text tool to add the words "HAPPY BIRTHDAY!" Try whichever font and colours you like. Use the select tool to position the text or trim the banner to fit.

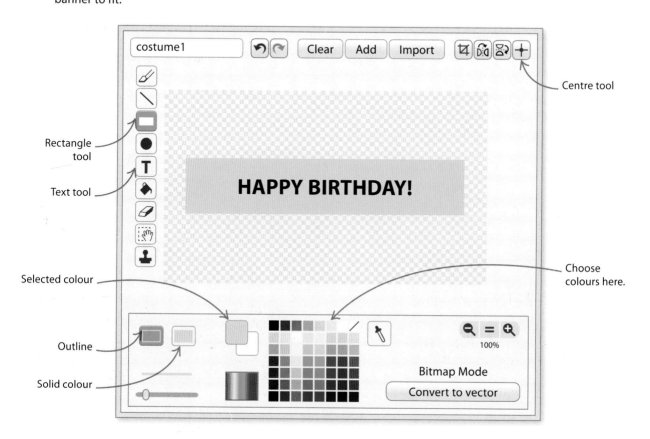

15 Click the centre tool ✛ in the top right of the paint editor and then click in the very centre of your banner. This is important as the banner's script will make it rotate around this point.

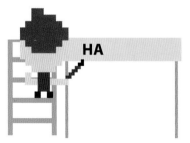

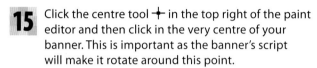

HAPPY BIRTHDAY!

Use this tool to set the costume's centre.

16 Now select the Scripts tab and add the banner's two scripts. These keep it hidden until the button is pressed and then jiggle the banner around. Run the project to check it works.

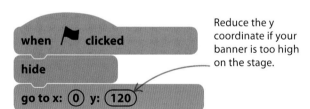

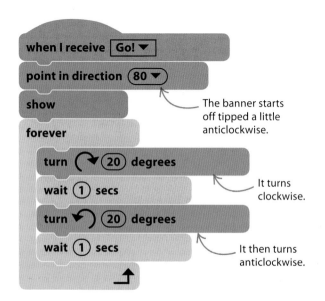

when 🏴 clicked
hide
go to x: (0) y: (120)

Reduce the y coordinate if your banner is too high on the stage.

when I receive [Go! ▼]
point in direction (80 ▼)
show
forever
　turn ↻ (20) degrees
　wait (1) secs
　turn ↺ (20) degrees
　wait (1) secs

The banner starts off tipped a little anticlockwise.

It turns clockwise.

It then turns anticlockwise.

Directions

Scratch uses degrees to set the direction of sprites. You can choose any number from –179° to 180°. Remember, negative numbers point sprites left and positive numbers point them right. Use 0° to go straight up and 180° to go straight down.

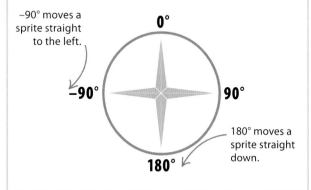

–90° moves a sprite straight to the left.

0°

–90°　90°

180°

180° moves a sprite straight down.

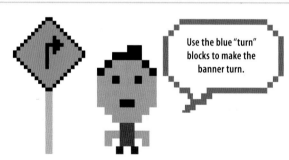

Use the blue "turn" blocks to make the banner turn.

Singing sharks

What's the perfect finishing touch to a birthday surprise? Yes, of course… singing sharks! The two sharks will take turns singing by sending messages to each other after each line of the song.

17 Click the sprite symbol ♠ in the sprites list and add the shark sprite to the project. You'll need two sharks, so rename the first one Shark1 by clicking on the sprite's "i" symbol.

Click here to rename the sprite.

18 To create the second shark, right-click (or control-click) on the first shark and select "duplicate". The new sprite will be named Shark2 automatically.

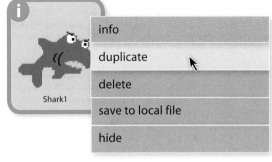

info

duplicate

delete

save to local file

hide

19 Now give Shark1 this script. When the project runs, Shark1 is hidden but takes its position in the top left of the stage. When it receives the "Go!" message, it reveals itself and glides down to the bottom of the stage.

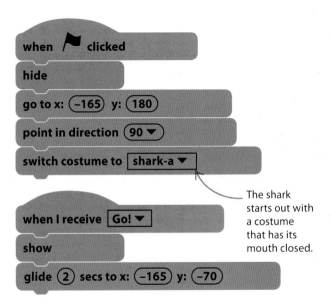

The shark starts out with a costume that has its mouth closed.

20 Add this script to Shark2. Run the project to test the sharks.

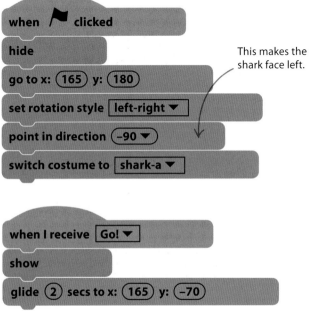

This makes the shark face left.

21 Time to get the sharks singing. Remember the loop belonging to the cake sprite that plays Happy Birthday? It sends the message "Line1" every time the song starts. Add the scripts shown on the left to Shark1 and the scripts on the right to Shark2 to make them react to the message. More messages make them take turns to sing each line. You'll need to create new messages for each line of the song. Name them by using the drop-down menu in the "broadcast" blocks.

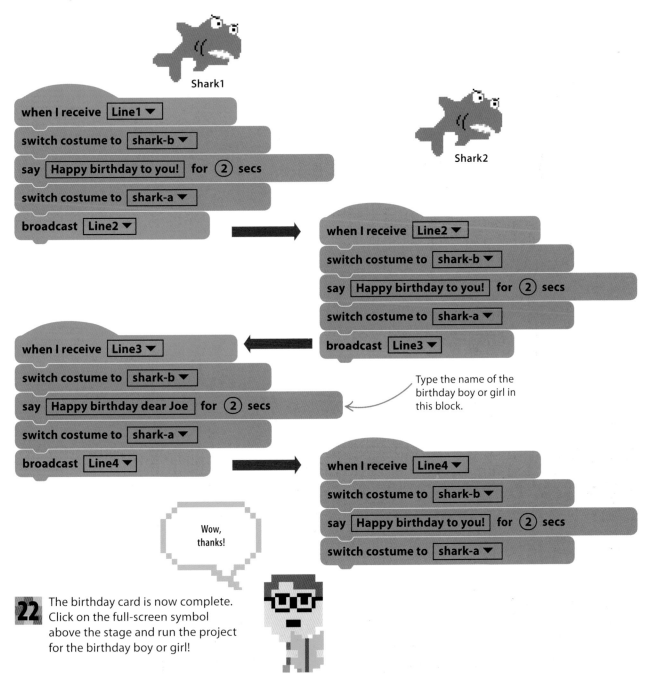

Shark1

when I receive Line1 ▼
switch costume to shark-b ▼
say Happy birthday to you! for 2 secs
switch costume to shark-a ▼
broadcast Line2 ▼

Shark2

when I receive Line2 ▼
switch costume to shark-b ▼
say Happy birthday to you! for 2 secs
switch costume to shark-a ▼
broadcast Line3 ▼

when I receive Line3 ▼
switch costume to shark-b ▼
say Happy birthday dear Joe for 2 secs
switch costume to shark-a ▼
broadcast Line4 ▼

Type the name of the birthday boy or girl in this block.

when I receive Line4 ▼
switch costume to shark-b ▼
say Happy birthday to you! for 2 secs
switch costume to shark-a ▼

Wow, thanks!

22 The birthday card is now complete. Click on the full-screen symbol above the stage and run the project for the birthday boy or girl!

Hacks and tweaks

You can customize your card for different people and occasions. Instead of using singing sharks, you could try singing lions, penguins, elephants, or ghosts. Change the song to "Merry Christmas" or "Jingle Bells" and replace the balloons with snowy Christmas trees if you like. Feel free to experiment.

▽ **Fading in**

The sharks drop from the top when they appear, but you can use Scratch's special effects to create a more dramatic entrance. To make an invisible sprite fade in slowly, for instance, use the "set ghost effect" block in the script shown here.

▽ **Supersize your sprite**

Another way to make a dramatic entrance is to start tiny and grow into a giant. Put a "change size by" block in a "repeat" loop to create this effect. You could also try making your sprite spin as it grows, or add a "change whirl effect" block to turn it into a crazy whirlpool.

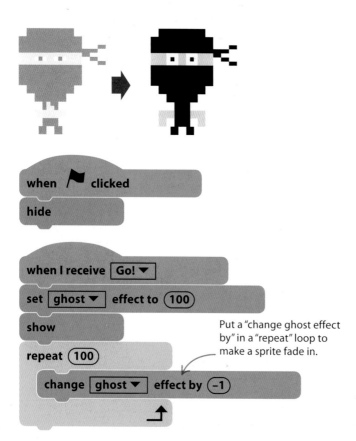

Put a "change ghost effect by" in a "repeat" loop to make a sprite fade in.

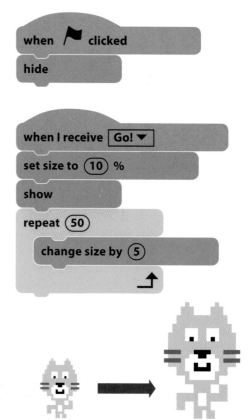

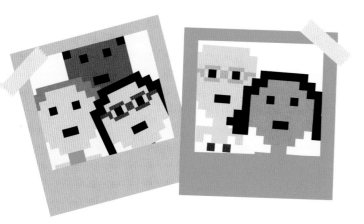

△ Adding photos

Why not try importing a photo of the birthday boy or girl into the project? You can upload any picture you like to make a new sprite by clicking the upload symbol ⬆ in the sprites list. But don't share projects containing people's photos without their permission.

· · TRY THIS

Sharks on elastic!

See if you can work out how to make the sharks move up at the end of the "Happy Birthday" song and then come back down when it's time to sing again. Don't forget to work on a separate copy of your project so you won't lose the original if things go wrong.

Scripts | Costumes | Sounds

New sound:

🔊 🎤 ⬆

Record a sound — Upload a sound

△ Adding sound

You don't have to use Scratch's built-in sounds and songs – you can add your own music or record your very own version of "Happy Birthday" if you want. Click the upload symbol ⬆ in the Sounds tab to add a sound file from your computer. Click the microphone symbol 🎤 to record your own sounds.

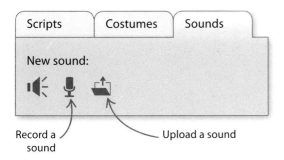

△ Birthday dancers

Why not reuse some of your dancers from the Dino Dance Party in your birthday card? If you do, adjust the timing of the costume change so they dance in time to the music.

Spiralizer

Try out this spinning spiral project. Change the patterns using special sliders to alter the values of variables in the code. You control the art – the possibilities are endless!

How it works

This simple project has only one sprite: a coloured ball, which stays in the middle. Scratch's clone blocks make copies of the ball that move outwards in straight lines. A spiral pattern forms because each clone moves in a slightly different direction, like water from a garden sprinkler. The Scratch pen draws a trail behind each clone, making colourful background patterns.

Click the icon to make the spiral fill your screen.

Spiralizer
by SpiralAttack (unshared)

Angle   10

Speed   2

Adjust the sliders to change the look of the spiral.

Each line is drawn using Scratch's built-in pen, which lets any sprite draw.

Each cloned ball flies in a straight line from the centre to the edge.

Wow! This project has got me in a spin.

The clones' different directions make them form a spiral.

The ball in the centre is the original sprite; all the others are clones.

△ **Clones**
Clones are working copies of sprites. When a clone is created, it appears on top of the existing sprite and has the same properties, such as direction, size, and so on.

△ **Scratch pen**
Every sprite can draw a trail behind it wherever it goes – just add the dark green "pen down" block to its script. Try out the other blocks in the Pen section of the blocks palette to change the pen's colour, shade, and thickness.

Ball clones

Scratch allows you to create hundreds of clones from a single sprite, filling the stage with action. Each clone is a fully working copy of the original sprite but also runs a special script that only affects clones.

1 Start a new project. Remove the cat sprite by right-clicking on it and selecting "delete". Load the ball sprite from the sprite library. The ball has several different coloured costumes. Click the Costumes tab and choose the colour you like best.

Ball

2 Add this loop to make clones of the ball. When you run this script nothing much will appear to happen. Actually, it's making lots of clones of the ball sprite, but they're all on top of each other. You can drag them apart with the mouse (but only in editor mode, not full-screen mode).

3 To make the clones move, add this second script to the ball sprite. Every new clone will now run its own copy of this script when it appears. The script makes the clone move away from the centre in the direction the parent sprite was pointing when it was cloned. Run the project.

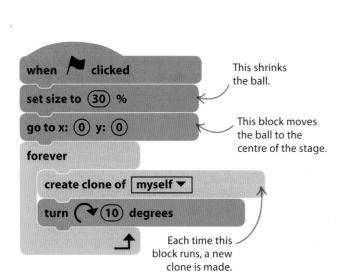

This shrinks the ball.

This block moves the ball to the centre of the stage.

Each time this block runs, a new clone is made.

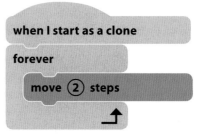

▷ **What's going on?**
The parent sprite changes its direction a little before each clone is created. As a result, the clones move off in slightly different directions, one after another. Each clone travels in a straight line to the edge of the stage, making the clones form an ever-expanding spiral pattern.

4 The clones will stop appearing after a while as Scratch won't allow more than 300 clones on the stage at once. Any instructions to make new clones after this are ignored. The clones stop forming at the centre and all the existing clones collect around the edge of the stage.

Spiralizer
by SpiralAttack (unshared)

The clones collect at the edge because the "move" block can't take a sprite completely off the stage.

Once there are 300 clones on the stage, no more clones are created.

5 To fix this problem, add an "if then" block inside the clone's "move" loop to delete the clone when it gets to the edge. Run this version. Now the balls should disappear at the edge as fast as they are made, and the spiral should continue for as long as you want – Scratch will never reach its clone limit.

6 To make the spiral show up better, add a black background. Click the paint symbol ✏ in the stage info area to the left of the sprites list to create a new backdrop. Use the fill tool to paint the backdrop solid black.

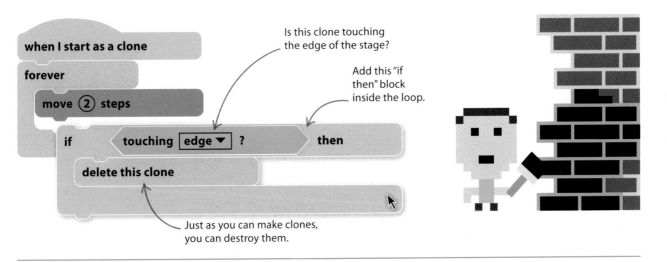

Is this clone touching the edge of the stage?

Add this "if then" block inside the loop.

```
when I start as a clone
forever
    move (2) steps
    if  < touching  edge ▼  ? >  then
        delete this clone
```

Just as you can make clones, you can destroy them.

Taking control

There are two numbers in the ball's scripts that you can change to alter the spiral's appearance. One is the change in the angle before each new clone appears. The other is the number of steps in the "move" block, which determines the clones' speed. If you create variables for these numbers, Scratch lets you add a slider control to the stage so you can change them while the project is running. This makes experimenting easy.

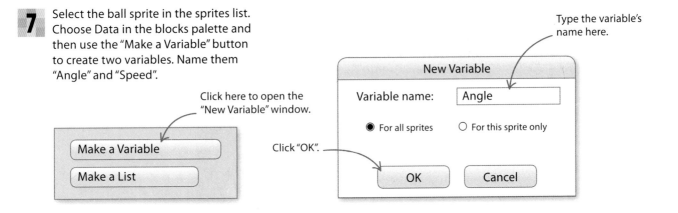

7 Select the ball sprite in the sprites list. Choose Data in the blocks palette and then use the "Make a Variable" button to create two variables. Name them "Angle" and "Speed".

Click here to open the "New Variable" window.

```
Make a Variable
Make a List
```

Type the variable's name here.

New Variable

Variable name: Angle

● For all sprites   ○ For this sprite only

Click "OK".

OK   Cancel

8 Keep the variables ticked in the blocks palette so that they appear on the stage.

The variables are shown on the stage like this.

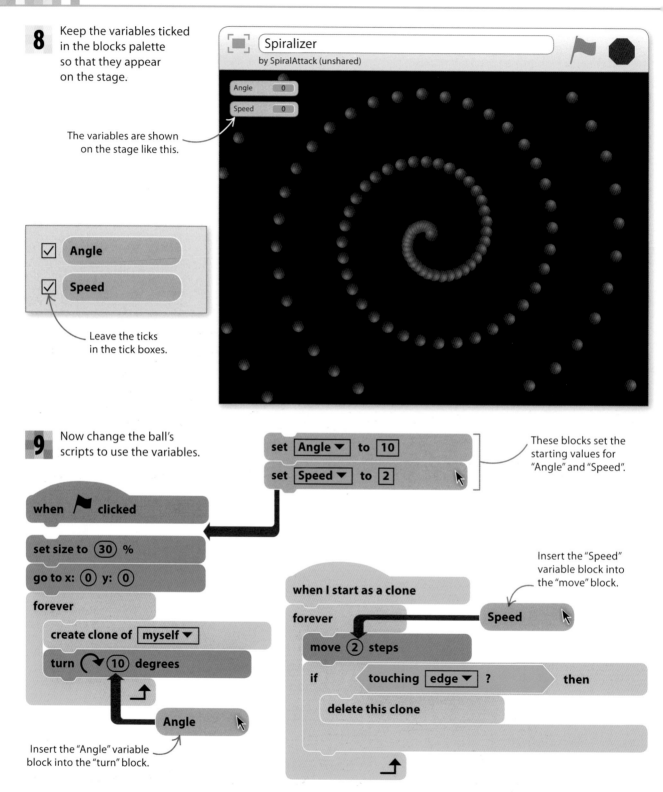

Spiralizer
by SpiralAttack (unshared)

Angle 0
Speed 0

☑ **Angle**

☑ **Speed**

Leave the ticks in the tick boxes.

9 Now change the ball's scripts to use the variables.

set Angle ▼ to 10
set Speed ▼ to 2

These blocks set the starting values for "Angle" and "Speed".

when 🏴 clicked

set size to (30) %

go to x: (0) y: (0)

forever

create clone of myself ▼

turn ↻ (10) degrees

Angle

Insert the "Angle" variable block into the "turn" block.

when I start as a clone

forever

move (2) steps

if touching edge ▼ ? then

delete this clone

Speed

Insert the "Speed" variable block into the "move" block.

10 Run the project and everything should work just as before. Right-click on the "Angle" variable on the stage and select "slider". Do the same for "Speed".

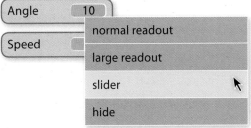

11 Both variables will now have a slider control. The sliders let you instantly change the values stored in the variables. Run the project and try moving the sliders. The patterns of the ball clones will change instantly.

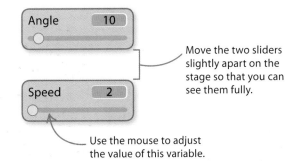

Move the two sliders slightly apart on the stage so that you can see them fully.

Use the mouse to adjust the value of this variable.

12 Now try experimenting with different values.

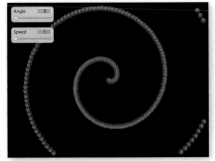

Angle 3, Speed 1

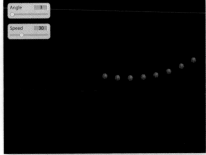

Angle 3, Speed 30

Angle 49, Speed 5

When the space-bar is pressed, every clone runs this script and deletes itself.

13 You might find it handy to clear the stage of clones from time to time, so add this script to turn the space-bar into a clone destroyer. Each clone runs all the ball sprite's scripts except the one headed by a green flag, so this script will affect every clone. Run the project and tap the space-bar to try it out.

```
when  space ▼  key pressed
delete this clone
```

The mighty pen

Every sprite in Scratch has a magic pen built in. If you switch the pen on, it will draw a line wherever the sprite goes. Every clone has a pen too, so by turning them on you can create some amazing art in our spiral project.

14 If you activate the pen for the original sprite, it will be activated for every clone (clones inherit everything from the parent sprite the moment they're created, such as size, direction, colour, costume, and so on). Add these green blocks to activate the pen for every clone.

when ⚑ clicked

set Angle ▼ to 7

set Speed ▼ to 2

set size to 30 %

go to x: 0 y: 0

This block removes all pen trails so the stage starts blank.

clear

This activates the pen so that every clone leaves a trail.

set pen size to 1

pen down

Type 1 in here for a thin pen.

forever

create clone of myself ▼

turn ↻ Angle degrees

15 Run the project to see a beautiful display. You can use the sliders to try different numbers. Odd numbers work well for "Angle" – try 7 or 11 – because the whole pattern moves around a little each time, filling the space and creating interesting effects.

When many lines are drawn close to each other, imperfections line up and make strange swirls called Moiré patterns.

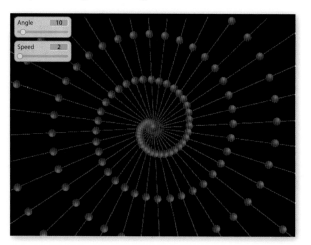

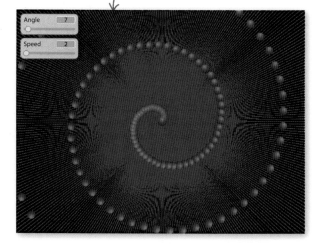

16 Add a "clear" block to your clone-destroyer script. This makes the space-bar wipe the stage clear of everything, creating a blank canvas for your art.

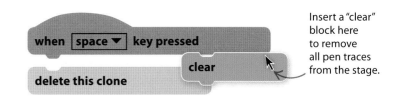

when `space ▼` key pressed

clear

delete this clone

Insert a "clear" block here to remove all pen traces from the stage.

17 As a final experiment, change the pen colour for each clone so that each one draws in a new colour.

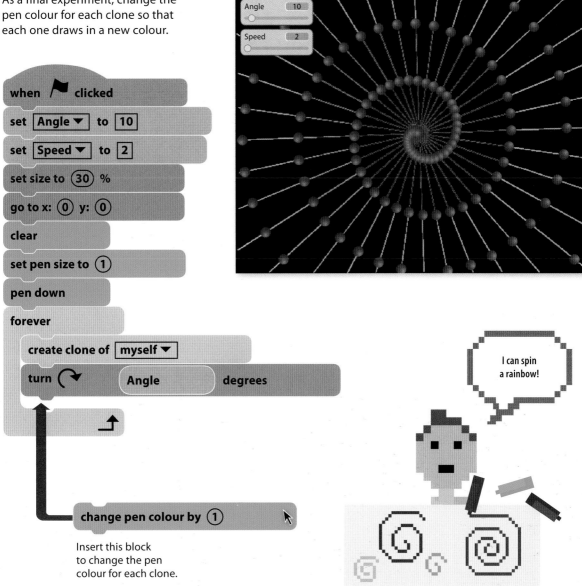

when 🏳 clicked

set `Angle ▼` to `10`

set `Speed ▼` to `2`

set size to `30` %

go to x: `0` y: `0`

clear

set pen size to `1`

pen down

forever

create clone of `myself ▼`

turn ↻ `Angle` degrees

change pen colour by `1`

Insert this block to change the pen colour for each clone.

Angle `10`
Speed `2`

I can spin a rainbow!

18 Run the project and explore the range of effects you can create by changing the sliders, the pen size, and the pen's colour change. Try thicker pen sizes and see what happens. Don't forget you can clear up by pressing the space-bar.

Play with the sliders to see what stunning visual effects you can make.

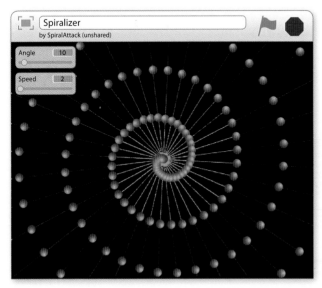

Pen size = 1, Angle = 10, Speed = 2

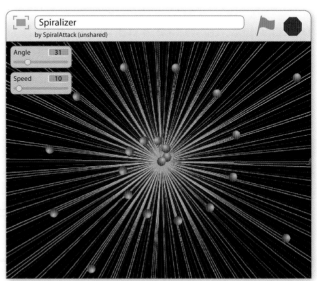

Pen size = 1, Angle = 31, Speed = 10

Pen size = 10, Angle = 10, Speed = 2

Pen size = 100, Angle = 10, Speed = 2

Hacks and tweaks

The spiral generator is perfect for customizing. Here are some more suggestions for changes, but don't be afraid to experiment with the code and try your own ideas. You could even adapt the project to make a game in which the player's sprite has to dodge the flying balls.

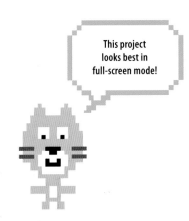

This project looks best in full-screen mode!

▷ Colour control

You could make a new variable, "PenChange", with its own slider (as in step 10) to control how quickly the lines change colour. Insert the new variable block in the "change pen colour" block. Then right-click on the slider to set the range. (If you give the "Angle" slider a negative minimum, you'll be able to reverse the spiral's direction.)

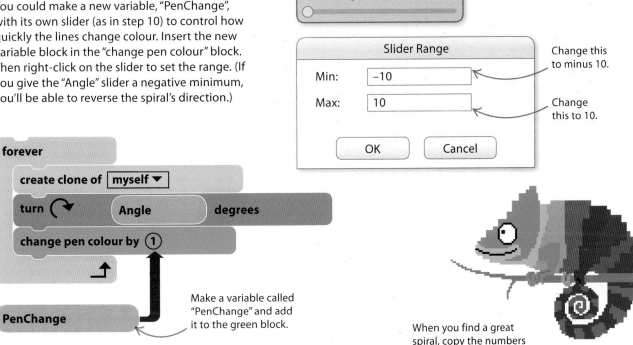

PenChange   0

Slider Range

Min: −10

Max: 10

OK   Cancel

Change this to minus 10.

Change this to 10.

```
forever
    create clone of myself ▼
    turn ↻ Angle degrees
    change pen colour by (1)
```

Make a variable called "PenChange" and add it to the green block.

PenChange

When you find a great spiral, copy the numbers from the sliders to make your preset code.

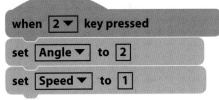

▷ Favourites

You can create keyboard shortcuts to set the spiral's variables to your favourite patterns. Then simply hit the keyboard shortcut to show someone your most dramatic creations.

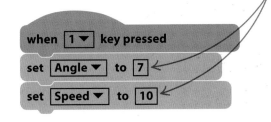

```
when 1 ▼ key pressed
set Angle ▼ to 7
set Speed ▼ to 10
```

```
when 2 ▼ key pressed
set Angle ▼ to 2
set Speed ▼ to 1
```

▽ Turn it into art

Add these scripts to hide the balls and sliders when you press the down arrow key and bring them back with the up arrow key. You can save the picture as an image file on your computer by right-clicking on the stage.

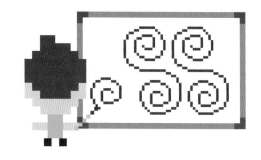

```
when down arrow ▼ key pressed
hide
hide variable Angle ▼
hide variable Speed ▼
```

This block hides all the clones.

These hide the sliders.

```
when up arrow ▼ key pressed
show
show variable Angle ▼
show variable Speed ▼
```

Remember that these scripts run for all the clones on the stage.

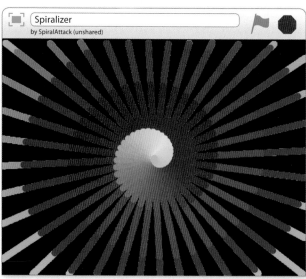

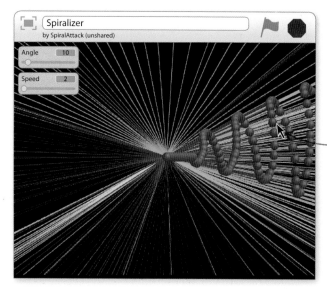

◁ Ball control

Instead of generating clones in a spiral pattern, you can make them follow the mouse-pointer. Just replace the "turn" block with a "point towards mouse-pointer" block. Now try painting with the mouse.

Clones shoot out from the centre towards the mouse-pointer.

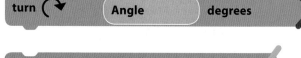

```
turn ↻   Angle   degrees        ✗

point towards mouse-pointer ▼    ✓
```

▷ **Sunset**

You can drag the original ball sprite anywhere on the stage and then hit the space-bar to clear the old pattern. See if you can create the artificial sunset pattern shown here. Hint: you'll need a pen size of 1 and the "Angle" variable set to 7. Don't forget there's a "go to" block in the code that will reset the position each time the project is run – you can take that block out or change the coordinates once you've found a good sun position. You could even add another full-sized ball sprite in yellow to be the sun.

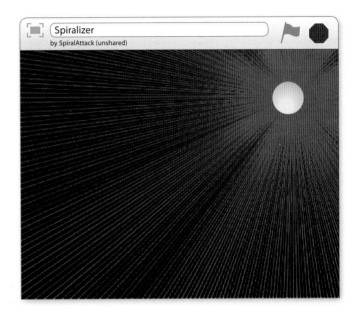

· · ▪ TRY THIS

Clone lab

Experiment with clones to get a feel for how they work. Start a new project and add a clone creation loop to the cat and give each clone a simple script to run when it starts. Experiment with a "pen down" block or put random numbers in a "go to x: y:" block to see some crazy effects. You can even add some keyboard controls and sound effects for fun. Once you've mastered clones, you'll find you can do all sorts of things in Scratch that are almost impossible without them.

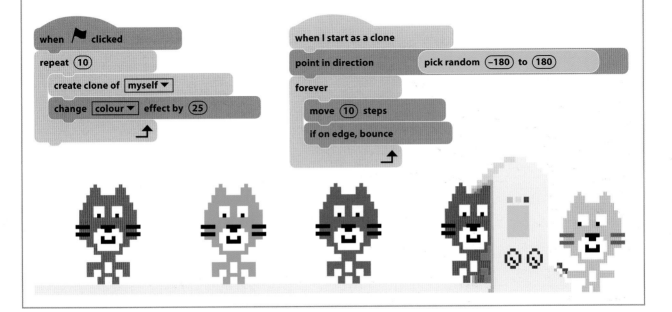

Fantastic Flowers

Create a virtual meadow and fill it with colourful flowers. In this project, you'll learn how to make your own customized Scratch blocks. Each time one of these runs, it triggers a special script called a subprogram, which paints a flower.

How it works

When you run the project, a flower appears wherever you click the mouse. Scratch uses a simple ball sprite and a "stamp" block to draw each flower. The ball stamps an image of itself to create each petal, moving back and forth from the flower's centre each time.

△ **Subprograms**
Scratch lets you create your own custom blocks to trigger scripts that you've built. Then, instead of repeating the whole script each time you need it, you simply use the new block. Programmers use this trick all the time and call the reused code a subprogram.

△ **Adding inputs**
You can create blocks that have windows for inputting numbers or other information, like the example shown here, which lets you set the number of petals.

Type the name of the project here.

Fantastic Flowers
by Buttercup (unshared)

Each flower is created with a custom "draw flower" block.

Create your own backdrop for the flowers.

You can choose the colours and number of petals or randomize them.

Another custom block draws flower stalks.

I think it must be spring!

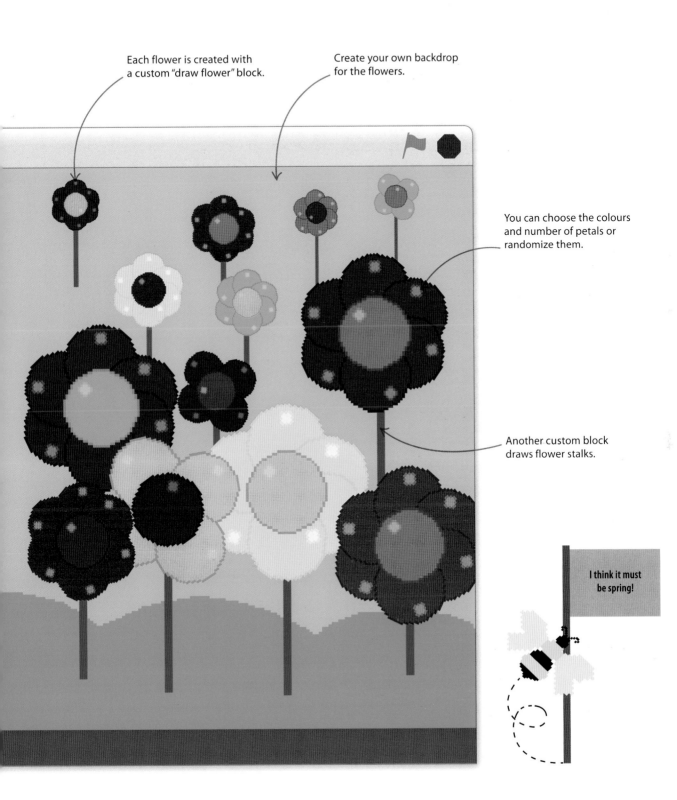

Make a flower

Follow these steps to make a script that creates a flower when you click on the stage. Once it's working, you can reuse the script to make the special flower-drawing block.

1 Start a new project. Remove the cat sprite by right-clicking on it and selecting "delete". Click on the sprite symbol ✿ and load the ball sprite from the sprite library. The ball is the building block for making each flower.

Ball

2 Build and run this script to draw a simple flower with five petals. The loop runs five times, drawing a ring of petals centred on the ball sprite's starting position. Each petal is a "stamp" image of the ball sprite.

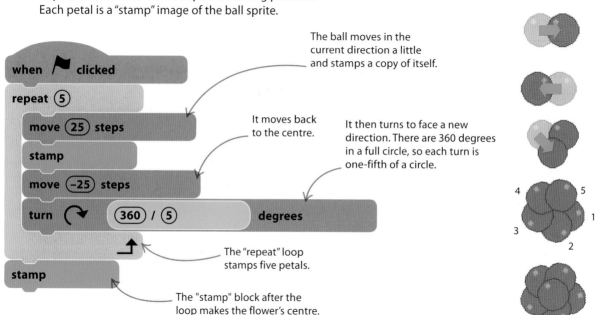

The ball moves in the current direction a little and stamps a copy of itself.

It moves back to the centre.

It then turns to face a new direction. There are 360 degrees in a full circle, so each turn is one-fifth of a circle.

The "repeat" loop stamps five petals.

The "stamp" block after the loop makes the flower's centre.

```
when [flag] clicked
repeat (5)
    move (25) steps
    stamp
    move (-25) steps
    turn ↻ (360) / (5) degrees
stamp
```

⸬ **EXPERT TIPS**

Doing maths

Computers are very good at maths. You can use the green Operators blocks in Scratch to do simple sums. For more complex calculations, you can also put Operators blocks inside each other or combine them with other blocks. If blocks are put inside each other, the computer works from the innermost blocks outwards, as if the inner blocks were in brackets.

Add
○ + ○

Subtract
○ − ○

Divide
○ / ○

○ * ○
Multiply (Computers usually use a * sign to avoid confusion with the letter x.)

More blocks

The next step is to turn the flower-drawing code into a flower-drawing block. You can then use this block to grow flowers wherever you want.

3 To make a new Scratch block, select More Blocks in the blocks palette and click "Make a Block". A window will open up. Type in the name of your new block: "draw flower".

Type the name of the new block here.

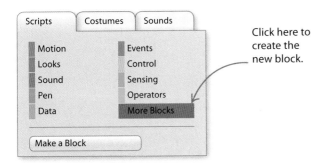

Click here to create the new block.

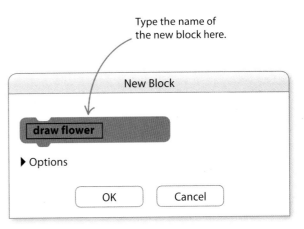

4 Once you've clicked "OK", you'll see the new block under More Blocks. Before you can use it, you'll need to create the script it will trigger (or "call", as programmers say).

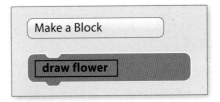

5 In the scripts area you'll see a new "define" header block with the same name as the block you've just created. Move the flower script under this header. The code will now run whenever the "draw flower" block runs.

when ⚑ clicked — Delete this block.

repeat **5**
  move **25** steps
  stamp
  move **-25** steps
  turn ↻ **360** / **5** degrees

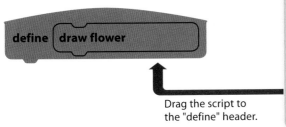

define draw flower

Drag the script to the "define" header.

stamp

6 Next, build a new script to use the "draw flower" block. When you run it, you can draw flowers with a click of your mouse.

7 Run the project and click around the stage to create a patch of flowers.

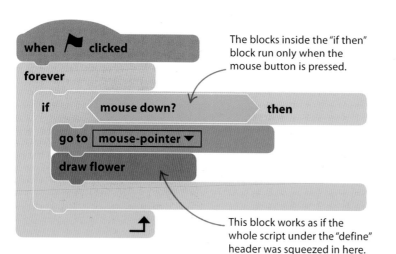

The blocks inside the "if then" block run only when the mouse button is pressed.

This block works as if the whole script under the "define" header was squeezed in here.

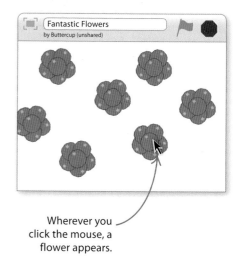

Wherever you click the mouse, a flower appears.

8 The stage will soon fill up, so make a flower-eraser script to clear away the flowers when you press the space-bar.

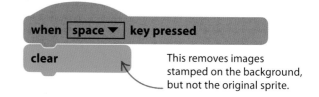

This removes images stamped on the background, but not the original sprite.

EXPERT TIPS

Subprograms

Good computer programmers always break up their programs into easily understandable chunks. Code that does something useful that you want to reuse within the program is moved into a "subprogram" and given a name. When the main script runs, or "calls", a subprogram, it's as if the code in the subprogram is inserted at that point. Using subprograms makes programs shorter, easier to understand, and simpler to change. Always give your custom blocks helpful names that describe what they do.

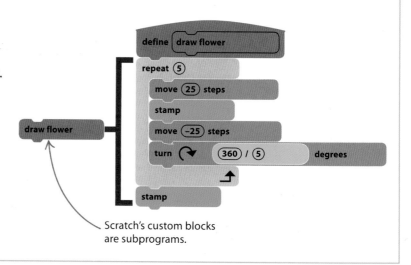

Scratch's custom blocks are subprograms.

Paint by numbers

If you wanted to make a lot of identical flowers, you could simply draw a flower sprite. The real power of custom blocks comes when you add inputs to them to change what they do. To make flowers of different colours with different numbers of petals, you can add input windows to the "draw flower" block.

9 To add an input window to control the number of petals in flowers, right-click (or control/shift-click) on the "define" header block and choose "edit".

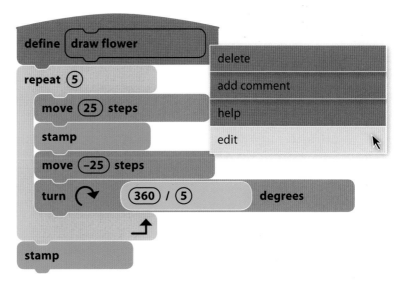

Choose this option.

10 A window will open up. Click on "Options" and then select the symbol next to "Add number input".

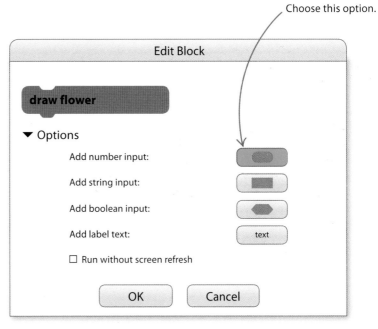

11 An input window now appears in the block. Type "number of petals" into this window and click "OK".

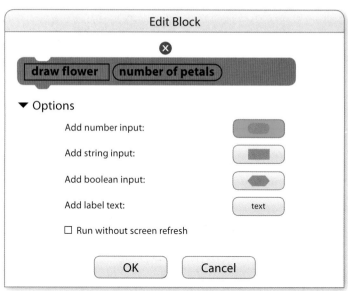

Edit Block

draw flower   number of petals

▼ Options

Add number input:	
Add string input:	
Add boolean input:	
Add label text:	text

☐ Run without screen refresh

OK   Cancel

12 You'll now see a dark blue "number of petals" block in the header block. You can drag copies of this off the header block and drop them in the script. Drag and drop copies into the "repeat" and "turn" blocks where the number of petals (5) is mentioned.

A new block appears inside the header block.

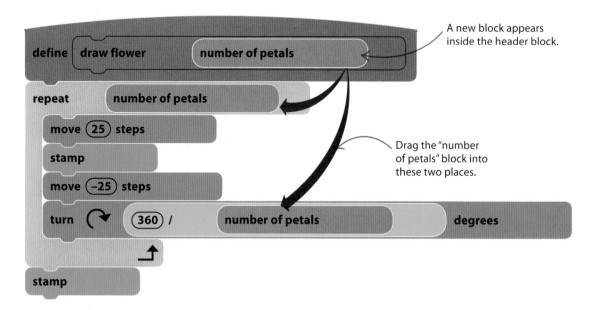

define   draw flower   number of petals

repeat   number of petals

move (25) steps

stamp

move (−25) steps

turn ↻ (360) / number of petals   degrees

stamp

Drag the "number of petals" block into these two places.

13 Look at the "draw flower" block in your script and you'll see that an input window has appeared. The number you type here will be used in the define script wherever "number of petals" appears. Type in the number seven.

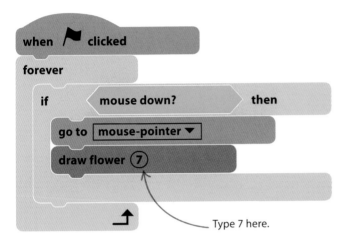

Type 7 here.

14 Run the project and click on the stage. Your flowers should have seven petals. Don't forget – you can clear the stage by pressing the space-bar.

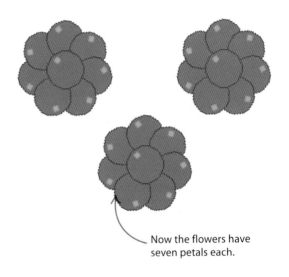

Now the flowers have seven petals each.

15 For more variety, insert a "pick random" block into the "draw flower" block instead of typing in the number of petals. Try it again.

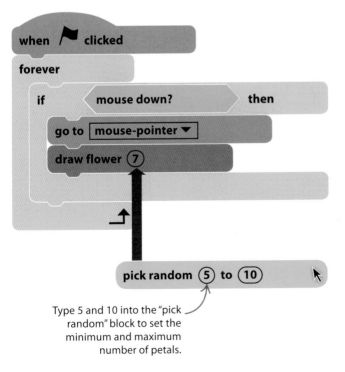

Type 5 and 10 into the "pick random" block to set the minimum and maximum number of petals.

16 Now add extra inputs to change the colour of the petals and the flower's centre. Right-click on the "define" block again, choose "edit", open "Options", and then add two number inputs called "petal colour" and "centre colour".

Click here if you want to delete an input window.

Edit Block

draw flower (number of petals) (petal colour) (centre colour)

▼ Options

Add number input:

Add string input:

Add boolean input:

Add label text: text

☐ Run without screen refresh

OK   Cancel

17 Add two new blocks to set the petal and flower-centre colours. Remember to drag the correct blue blocks onto these from the header.

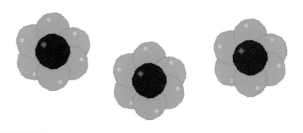

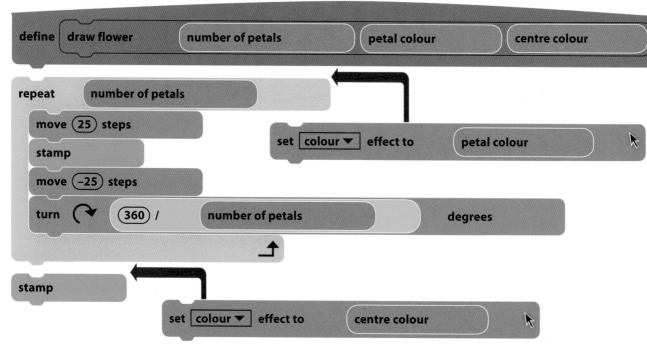

define draw flower | number of petals | petal colour | centre colour

repeat number of petals
move 25 steps
stamp
move −25 steps
turn ↻ 360 / number of petals degrees

set colour ▼ effect to petal colour

stamp

set colour ▼ effect to centre colour

18 Now add a "clear" block to the main script and type the numbers 6, 70, and 100 into the "draw flower" block to make six-petalled blue flowers. Run the project to check it works.

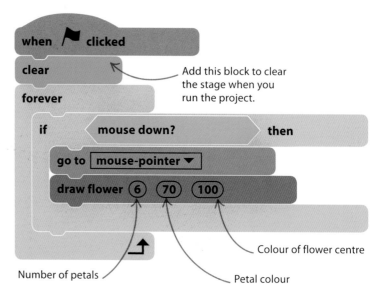

when ⚑ clicked
clear
forever
if mouse down? then
go to mouse-pointer ▼
draw flower 6 70 100

Add this block to clear the stage when you run the project.

Colour of flower centre

Number of petals

Petal colour

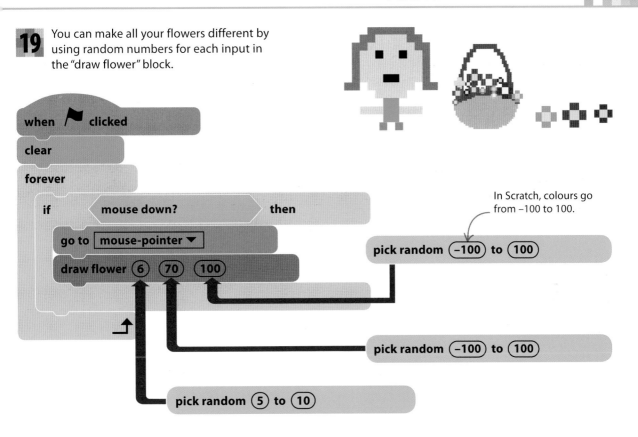

19 You can make all your flowers different by using random numbers for each input in the "draw flower" block.

```
when 🏳 clicked
clear
forever
    if  mouse down?  then
        go to  mouse-pointer ▼
        draw flower (6) (70) (100)
```

In Scratch, colours go from −100 to 100.

```
pick random (−100) to (100)
```

```
pick random (−100) to (100)
```

```
pick random (5) to (10)
```

20 Run the project and click around the stage to make a flower garden. Don't forget you can press the space-bar to clear the stage.

Don't forget to save your work from time to time if you use Scratch offline!

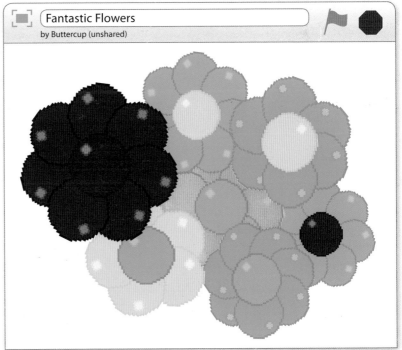

Fantastic Flowers
by Buttercup (unshared)

Flower stalks

Real flowers grow on stalks, so follow the next few steps to add stalks to your virtual flowers to make them look more realistic. Using custom blocks makes the code easy to read so you always know what's going on.

21 Choose More Blocks in the blocks palette and then click "Make a Block". Call the new block "draw stalk". After you've typed the name of the block, open the Options menu and add number inputs for the length and thickness of the stalk. Then click "OK".

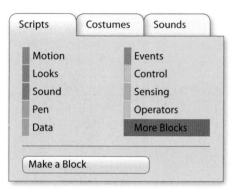

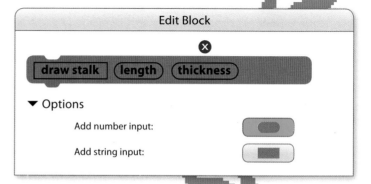

22 Build this script below the "define" header block. Drag the "length" and "thickness" blocks from the header to where they're used in the script.

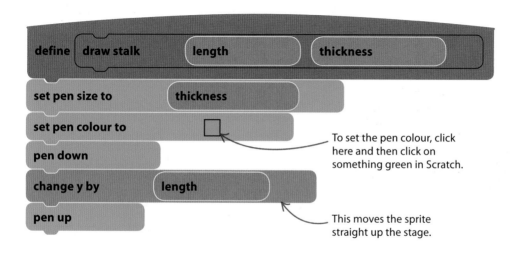

To set the pen colour, click here and then click on something green in Scratch.

This moves the sprite straight up the stage.

23 Next, add the new "draw stalk" block to the main script. Fill in the numbers to set the stalk's length to 100 and its thickness to 5.

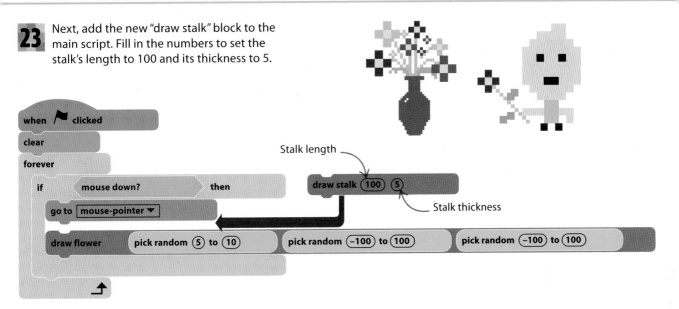

when ⚑ clicked

clear

forever

  if   mouse down?   then

    go to mouse-pointer ▼

    draw flower   pick random 5 to 10   pick random -100 to 100   pick random -100 to 100

Stalk length

draw stalk 100 5

Stalk thickness

24 Run the project. You can now make a whole meadow of coloured flowers. Experiment with different numbers in the "pick random" blocks to change the look of your flowers.

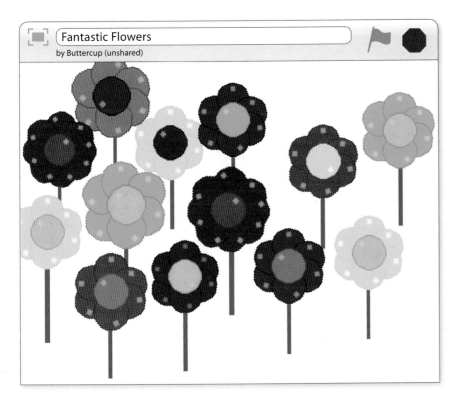

Fantastic Flowers
by Buttercup (unshared)

25 For a finishing touch, add a backdrop for your flower meadow. You can paint your own backdrop by clicking the paint symbol / to the left of the sprites list. Alternatively, click the backdrop symbol 🖼 to load one from the library.

2

blue sky
492x367

3

playing-field
480x360

Hacks and tweaks

Feel free to experiment with the code to change the colour, size, and shape of the flowers as much as you want. You don't have to use the ball sprite as the template – try creating your own templates to generate more interesting shapes. With a little imagination you can create all sorts of beautiful scenes.

Give your petal a coloured outline if you like.

▷ **Different petals**

Why not use the costume editor to add a different petal to the flowers? Click on the Costumes tab and add a new costume with the paint symbol ✏. Oval petals work well. You'll need to add blocks to the "define draw flower" script to swap between the petal costume and the ball-a costume for the flower's centre.

▽ **Flowers everywhere**

Try swapping the main script for this one. It draws flowers in random places automatically, eventually covering the stage with them. Think about how you could add position inputs to the "draw flower" block – you'd need to add x and y inputs and add a "go to" block at the start of the block's definition.

The chosen ranges keep the flowers away from the edges.

```
when ⚑ clicked
clear
forever
    go to x: pick random (-200) to (200)    y: pick random (-140) to (140)
    draw flower  pick random (5) to (10)    pick random (-100) to (100)    pick random (-100) to (100)
```

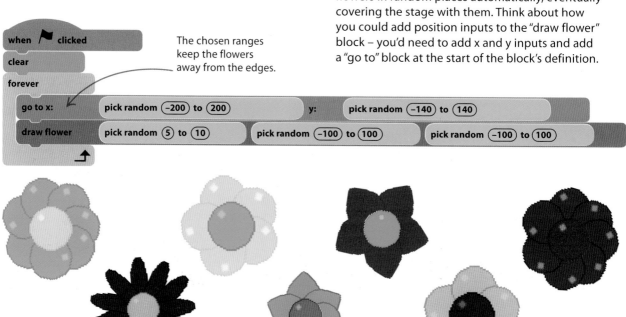

Different sizes

By adding another input to the "draw flower" block, you can control the size of your flowers. You can also make the meadow look more 3D by making the flowers smaller if they're near the top of the stage, as though further away.

1 Right-click the "define" header to edit it and add a new input called "scale". Make the changes shown below to the script. When scale is set to 100 in the "draw flower" block, the flowers are drawn at their usual size. Smaller numbers will produce smaller flowers.

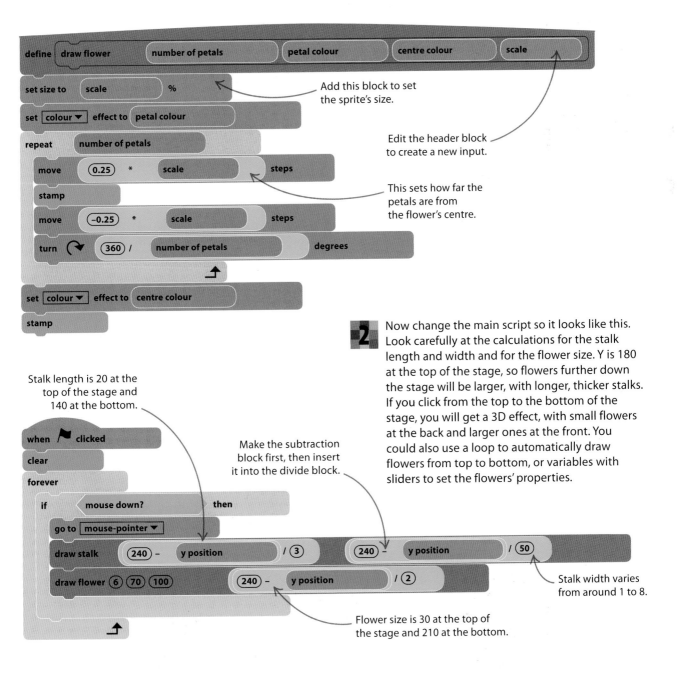

Add this block to set the sprite's size.

Edit the header block to create a new input.

This sets how far the petals are from the flower's centre.

2 Now change the main script so it looks like this. Look carefully at the calculations for the stalk length and width and for the flower size. Y is 180 at the top of the stage, so flowers further down the stage will be larger, with longer, thicker stalks. If you click from the top to the bottom of the stage, you will get a 3D effect, with small flowers at the back and larger ones at the front. You could also use a loop to automatically draw flowers from top to bottom, or variables with sliders to set the flowers' properties.

Stalk length is 20 at the top of the stage and 140 at the bottom.

Make the subtraction block first, then insert it into the divide block.

Stalk width varies from around 1 to 8.

Flower size is 30 at the top of the stage and 210 at the bottom.

Games

Tunnel of Doom

Scratch is the ideal playground for making and perfecting games. To win at this game, you need a steady hand and nerves of steel. Take the cat all the way through the Tunnel of Doom, but don't touch the walls! For an extra challenge, try to beat the best time.

The cat starts here.

Tunnel of Doom
by DirtDigger465 (unshared)

How it works

Use your mouse to move the cat all the way through the tunnel without touching the walls. If you accidentally touch a wall, you go back to the start. You can try as many times as you like, but the clock will keep counting the seconds until you finish.

◁ **Cat sprite**
Once the mouse-pointer has touched the cat, the cat follows it everywhere. You don't need to use the mouse button.

◁ **Tunnel**
The tunnel maze is a giant sprite that fills the stage. The tunnel itself isn't actually part of the sprite – it's a gap that you create by using the eraser tool in Scratch's paint editor. If the cat stays in the middle of the path, it won't be detected as touching the tunnel sprite.

◁ **Home**
When the cat touches the home sprite, the game ends with a celebration.

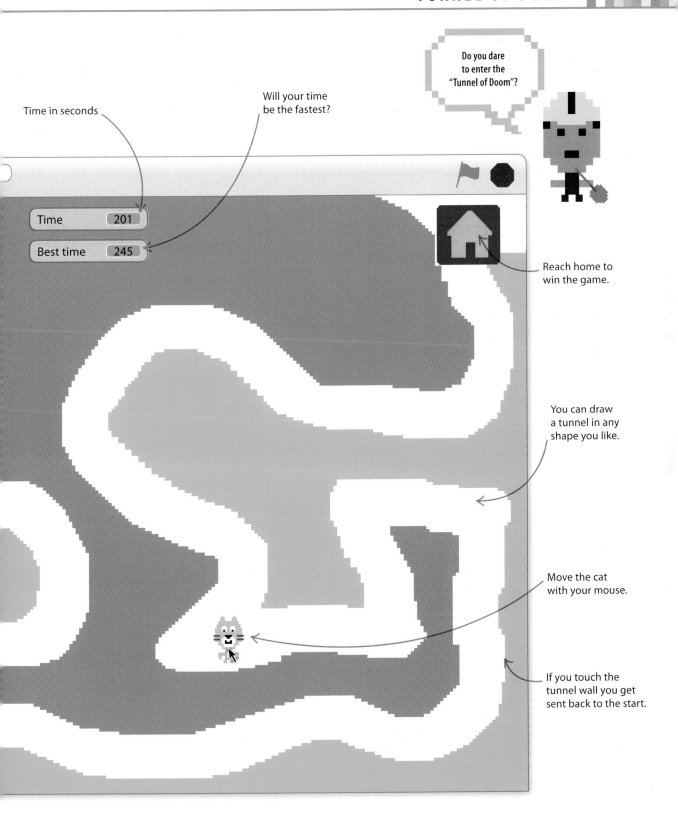

Do you dare to enter the "Tunnel of Doom"?

Time in seconds

Will your time be the fastest?

Time — 201

Best time — 245

Reach home to win the game.

You can draw a tunnel in any shape you like.

Move the cat with your mouse.

If you touch the tunnel wall you get sent back to the start.

Set the mood

Start by setting the scene for the game with some appropriate music. You can choose any music you like from the sound library in Scratch by following the steps below.

1 Start a new project. Let the cat sprite stay, but change its name from Sprite1 to Cat to keep things simple.

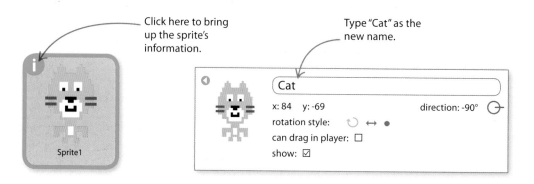

Click here to bring up the sprite's information.

Type "Cat" as the new name.

Cat

x: 84   y: -69   direction: -90°

rotation style:

can drag in player: ☐

show: ☑

Sprite1

2 Before building any scripts, add some music to create the right atmosphere for the game. Click on the Sounds tab above the blocks palette and then on the speaker symbol 🔊 to open the sound library. Now choose "Music Loops". To preview a sound, click the play symbol. When you find one you like, highlight its speaker symbol and click "OK".

Click here to see only the music sound clips that can be played over and over.

Click here to listen to a sound before you load it.

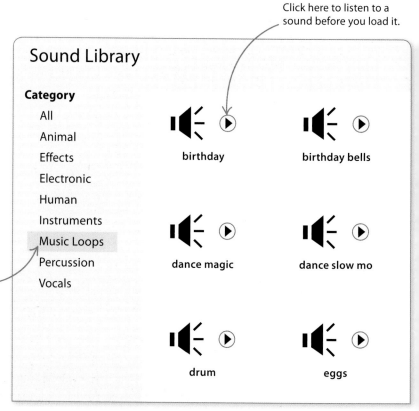

Sound Library

Category

All

Animal

Effects

Electronic

Human

Instruments

Music Loops

Percussion

Vocals

birthday

birthday bells

dance magic

dance slow mo

drum

eggs

3 Add this script to the cat sprite to loop the music. Use the "play sound _ until done" block, not "play sound _", otherwise things go wrong as Scratch tries to play your sound lots of times at once.

4 Now run the project and the music should play… forever. Click on the red stop button above the stage to stop it again.

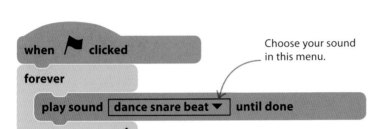

Choose your sound in this menu.

Creating the tunnel

The next step is to make the twisty tunnel that will challenge the player's nerve and steadiness of hand. How you draw the tunnel affects the difficulty of the game.

5 Click the paint symbol ✏ above the sprites list to create a new sprite with the paint editor. Choose a colour you like and click on the fill tool ◆. Then click anywhere in the paint area to fill it with a solid colour.

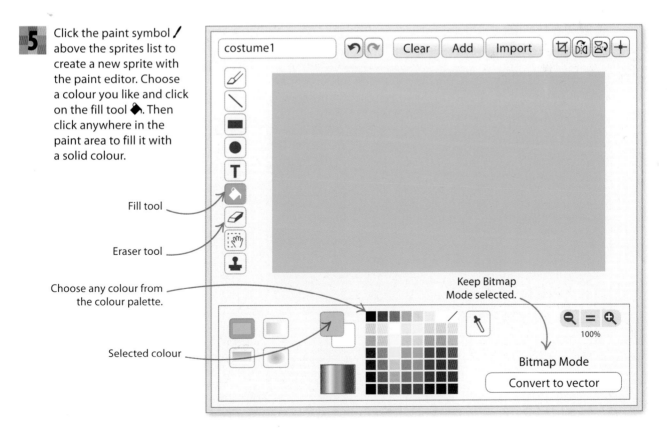

Fill tool

Eraser tool

Choose any colour from the colour palette.

Selected colour

Keep Bitmap Mode selected.

6 Now select the eraser tool and move the slider at the bottom left so it's nearly full size.

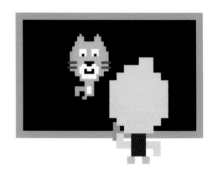

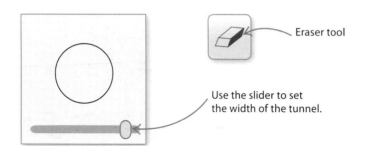

Eraser tool

Use the slider to set the width of the tunnel.

Start position   End position

7 Use the eraser to make gaps in the top left and top right where the maze starts and ends. Then draw a wiggly tunnel between the two corners. If things go wrong, click the undo symbol ↰ at the top and try again.

The tunnel should be chequered, not white.

8 To make the maze look more interesting, use the fill tool to paint the central area a different colour. Don't fill the tunnel with a colour or the game won't work.

Click in this area to fill it with a second colour.

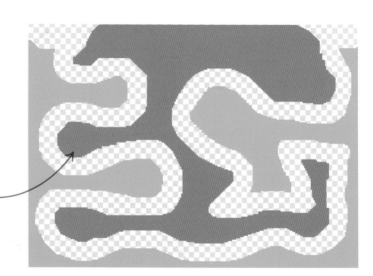

9 Now click on the blue "i" on this sprite in the sprites list and rename it "Tunnel".

10 With the tunnel sprite selected in the sprites list, click on the Scripts tab and build this script to position it correctly and to animate it. Run the project to test it.

Click here to bring up the sprite's information.

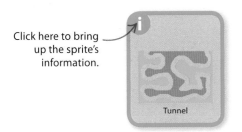

Tunnel

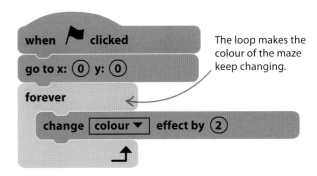

when ⚑ clicked

go to x: (0) y: (0)

forever

change colour ▼ effect by (2)

The loop makes the colour of the maze keep changing.

Mouse control

Now to add some scripts to the cat to turn the project into a working game. The scripts build step by step, so test them as you go along to check they work properly.

11 Select the cat sprite and add this script. It shrinks the cat and positions it at the start of the tunnel. Once the mouse-pointer touches the cat, it will move with the mouse. Note that players don't need to click on the cat to pick it up. The script stops with a "meow" if the cat touches the tunnel walls.

Choose a smaller size if the cat gets stuck too easily in the tunnel.

This stops the cat from disappearing behind the maze.

This sets the cat's start position in the top-left corner.

when ⚑ clicked

set size to (20) %

go to front

go to x: (-210) y: (160)

wait until ⟨ touching mouse-pointer ▼ ? ⟩

repeat until ⟨ touching Tunnel ▼ ? ⟩

go to mouse-pointer ▼

play sound meow ▼ until done

Nothing happens until the player's mouse-pointer touches the cat.

Repeat until loops

The useful "repeat until" loop repeats the blocks inside it until the condition at the top of the block becomes true, and then the blocks below are run. The block makes it easier to write simple, readable code, like this example.

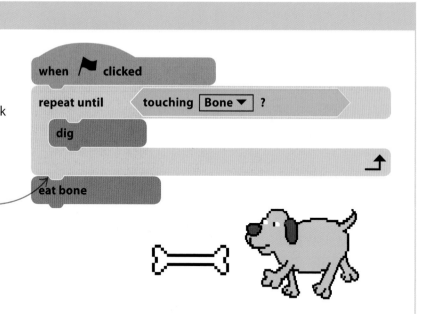

Unlike the "forever" block, "repeat until" has a bump at the bottom allowing more blocks to be added to it.

12 Run the game. You should be able to control the cat once you've touched it with your mouse-pointer. Try moving it along the tunnel. If you touch the wall, the cat will meow and get stuck. If the cat gets stuck too often, reduce the number in the "set size" block, but don't make it too easy.

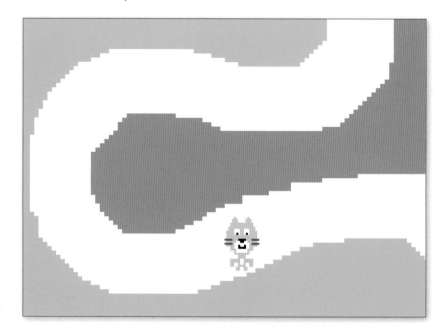

13 At the moment you have to restart the game if you touch the wall. Add this loop to the script to send the cat back to the start for another try if it touches the wall. Test the game again.

TRY AGAIN!

Drag the top of the "forever" block above the "go to" block and it will expand to fit around all the blocks below.

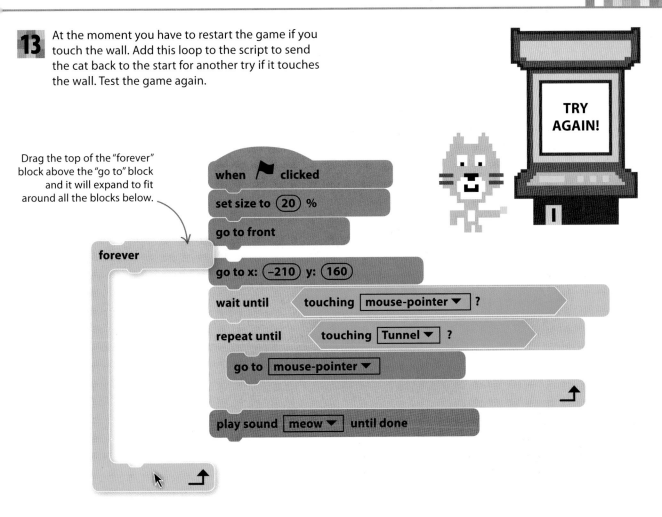

when ⚑ clicked

set size to (20) %

go to front

forever

go to x: (−210) y: (160)

wait until ⟨ touching [mouse-pointer ▼] ? ⟩

repeat until ⟨ touching [Tunnel ▼] ? ⟩

go to [mouse-pointer ▼]

play sound [meow ▼] until done

14 Click the sprite symbol ✿ above the sprites list to add a new sprite to the game. Choose the Home Button sprite and rename it "Home" in the sprites list. On the stage, drag it into the top-right corner.

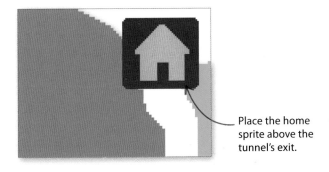

Place the home sprite above the tunnel's exit.

15 It will probably be too big, so add this script to shrink it. Run the project and reposition the house on the stage if you need to.

when ⚑ clicked

set size to (50) %

16 Next you need to add some code to check if the cat has made it home. Select the cat in the sprites list and add the blocks shown here. The blocks inside the "if then" block run only if the cat is touching the house.

Open the menu, create a new message, and call it "Well Done". You'll need it later.

This stops the music and a timer script that you'll add later.

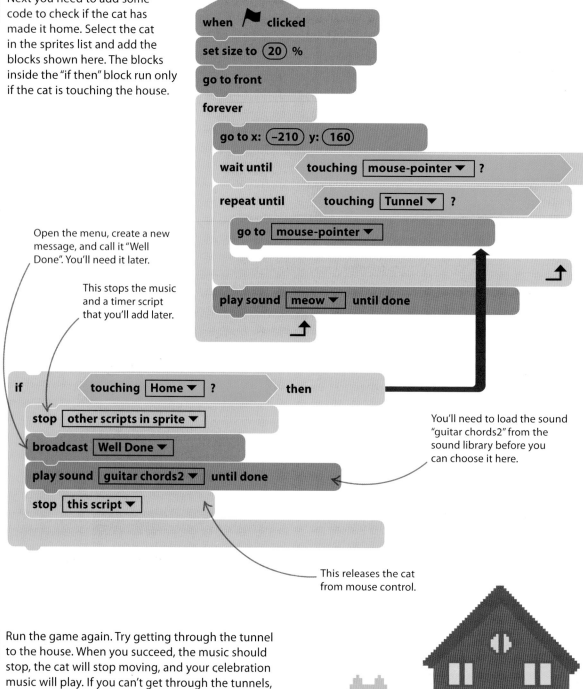

You'll need to load the sound "guitar chords2" from the sound library before you can choose it here.

This releases the cat from mouse control.

17 Run the game again. Try getting through the tunnel to the house. When you succeed, the music should stop, the cat will stop moving, and your celebration music will play. If you can't get through the tunnels, then you need to make the cat smaller, but you can test the game's end by clicking on the cat and dragging it home (this is cheating!).

Against the clock

Tunnel of Doom is more fun if you add a timer to show how quickly you've made it through the tunnel. Then you can challenge other players to beat your best time.

18 Click on Data in the blocks palette and make a variable called "Time". Leave the check box ticked so the variable is shown on the stage.

New Variable

Variable name: Time

● For all sprites   ○ For this sprite only

OK   Cancel

Type the name here.

19 Add this script to the cat. It simply counts the seconds since the game started. Move the "Time" variable to the top centre of the stage so the player can see it easily.

20 Try the game again. When you get the cat home the timer stops, leaving your final time displayed on the stage.

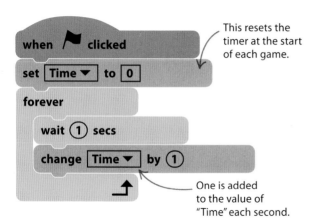

This resets the timer at the start of each game.

One is added to the value of "Time" each second.

Wow! That was a speedy escape.

21 To make winning the game feel more rewarding, add a new sprite to show a message congratulating the player. Click on the paint symbol ✏ above the sprites list to make a sign in the paint editor using coloured shapes and the text tool. The one shown here is just a suggestion – you can use your own ideas.

22 To set the centre of the sprite, click the centre tool ✛ at the top of the paint editor and then click in the very centre of your sign. When you use a "go to x: y:" block in Scratch, it puts the sprite's centre at the chosen coordinates.

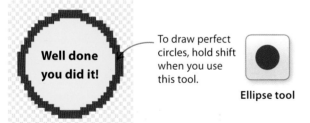

To draw perfect circles, hold shift when you use this tool.

Ellipse tool

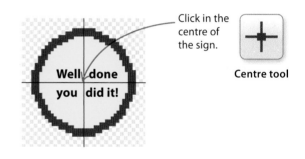

Click in the centre of the sign.

Centre tool

23 To make the sign work, add these scripts to your new sprite. The first one hides the sign when the project starts, and the second is triggered when the "Well Done" message is sent by the cat. It displays the sign and makes it flash.

24 Your game is now complete. Test it thoroughly (by playing lots) and then challenge your friends to see if they can beat your times.

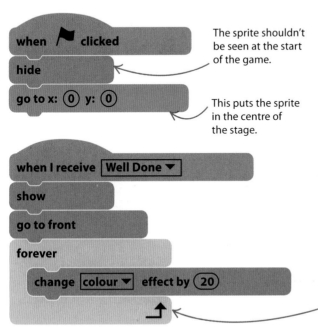

The sprite shouldn't be seen at the start of the game.

This puts the sprite in the centre of the stage.

Rapid colour changes make the sign flash.

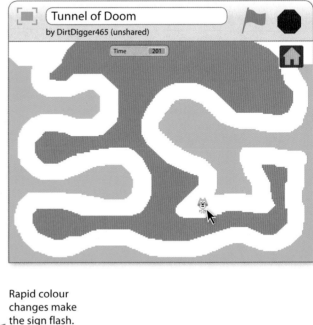

Tunnel of Doom
by DirtDigger465 (unshared)

Time 201

Hacks and tweaks

This game is bursting with possibilities. Save a copy and start experimenting! You could add extra sound effects or extra sprites, such as a floating ghost to scare the cat back to the start or a friendly bat that jumps the player to a later spot in the tunnel.

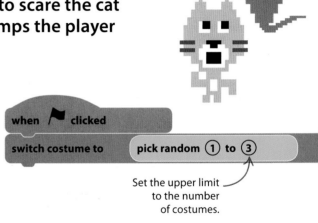

▷ **Let's twist again**
You can make the game harder or easier by changing how wide and twisty the tunnel is. You could also create tunnels with branches – perhaps make the player choose between a short narrow tunnel and a long wide one. You could even make several different costumes for the tunnel sprite and choose a random one at the start of each game by adding this script.

when ⚑ clicked

switch costume to   pick random ① to ③

Set the upper limit to the number of costumes.

▽ Best time

You can make the game show the best time achieved so far, like a high score. Make a new variable called "Best time" and drag it next to the "Time" display on the stage. Then add the script below to the cat to capture new best times when the cat gets home.

| Time | 35 |
| Best time | 15 |

The best time achieved is shown on the stage.

This block is true the first time you run the game.

True if your time was quicker than the old record.

```
when I receive  Well Done ▼

if      Best time      = 0     or      Time     <     Best time            then

    set  Best time ▼  to     Time
```

This block stores the last game's time as the new best time.

▽ Who's the best?

You can display the name of the quickest player by making another variable, "Best player", and showing it on the stage. Add these two blocks shown here to the best-time script.

I won! Let's celebrate!

```
when I receive  Well Done ▼

if      Best time      = 0     or      Time     <     Best time            then

    set  Best time ▼  to     Time
```

```
ask  What's your name?  and wait

set  Best player ▼  to     answer
```

This asks the player to give his or her name when there's a new best time.

Whatever the player types is stored in the "answer" block once.

Window Cleaner

Messy windows? You'd better get up and clean them! This frantic game counts how many splats you can clean off your computer screen in a minute. You can wipe away the splats either by using a computer mouse or by waving your hand in front of a webcam.

How it works

The game starts by cloning a splat sprite and scattering clones with different costumes randomly across the stage. When motion is detected by the webcam, Scratch uses its "ghost" effect to make the splats fade. If you wave your hand enough, they eventually disappear. The aim of the game is to remove as many splats as you can in one minute.

▽ **Splat sprite**
This game has one sprite with several costumes, which you'll paint yourself. By cloning the sprite you can cover the screen with splats of messy gunk.

Window Cleaner
by PaintChampion (unshared)

Score 42

Countdown 8

Each splat is a clone of the project's single sprite.

Wave your hand to rub out the splats.

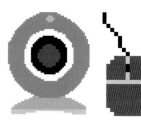

△ **Controls**
First you'll clean up the splats with your mouse, but later you can change the code to detect the movement of your hand with a webcam.

Slime time!

To make some mess on the screen, you need to draw some slimy splats. Follow these instructions and you'll be in a mess in no time at all.

1 Start a new project. Remove the cat sprite by right-clicking (or control/shift-clicking) on it and selecting "delete". Click on the paint symbol ╱ in the sprites list to paint a new sprite.

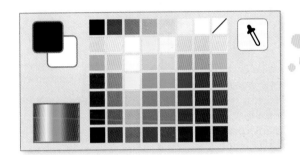

2 The paint editor will open. To make your first splat, choose a colour from the palette.

3 Select the brush tool and draw the outline of a large splat. Use the whole paint area as it will get shrunk later.

Brush tool

Yay! This is more fun than paintball!

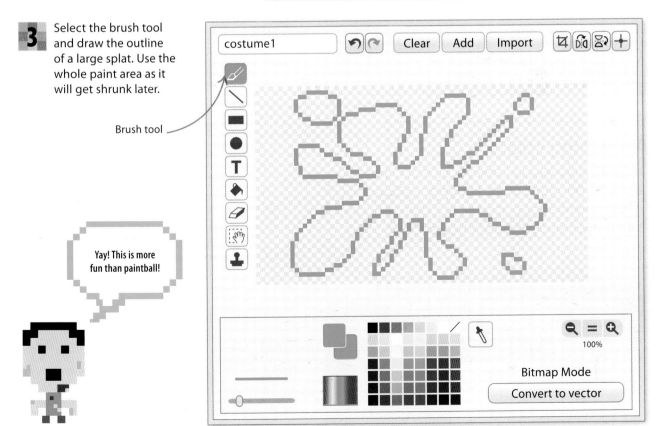

9 Run the game to test it. Ten splats should appear. You should be able to remove the splats by touching them with the mouse-pointer, but new splats will appear too. However, there's a problem – the game never comes to an end.

Goodbye splat!

Countdown

Nothing puts a player under pressure like a time limit. The next script will give the player a one-minute countdown in which to zap as many splats as they can.

10 Make a new variable and call it "Countdown". This will tell the player how much time they have left. Keep it ticked so it appears on the stage.

☑ **Countdown**

11 Add this script to launch the countdown. Once the timer has ticked down, it stops the other script from making any more splats and sends out a message that you'll need later on.

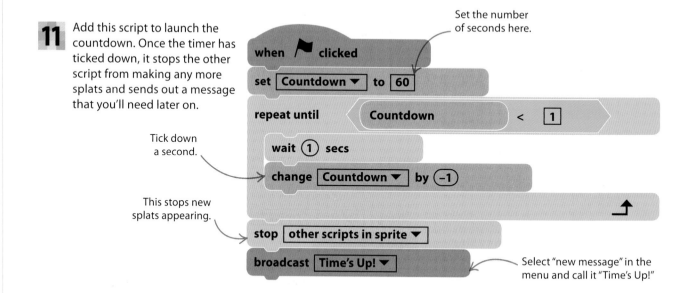

Set the number of seconds here.

Tick down a second.

This stops new splats appearing.

Select "new message" in the menu and call it "Time's Up!"

12 Test the game. It should end when the timer reaches zero. But there's a small problem: any leftover splats can still be cleaned up for points, even though the game's over. To prevent this, add this tiny script to remove any remaining splats. Now try the game again.

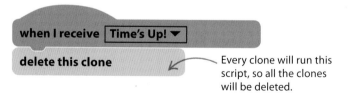

Every clone will run this script, so all the clones will be deleted.

Camera control

You can make the window cleaning more realistic by adding camera controls. You'll need a webcam attached to your computer to complete the next section. When playing the game with the webcam, stand well back from the computer screen so that most of your body is visible on the stage.

13 Make a new variable and call it "Difficulty". This can be set anywhere from 0 to 100 – the higher the number, the harder the game. Uncheck the tick box so the variable isn't shown on the stage.

☐ **Difficulty**

14 Add this script to set the value of "Difficulty" and turn on the webcam. Try setting "Difficulty" to 40 to start with. You can adjust the value later if the lighting and background in your room make the game too easy or hard. Don't run the game yet.

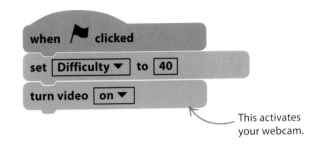

This activates your webcam.

15 To use the camera to delete the splats instead of the mouse, change the "when I start as a clone" script like this.

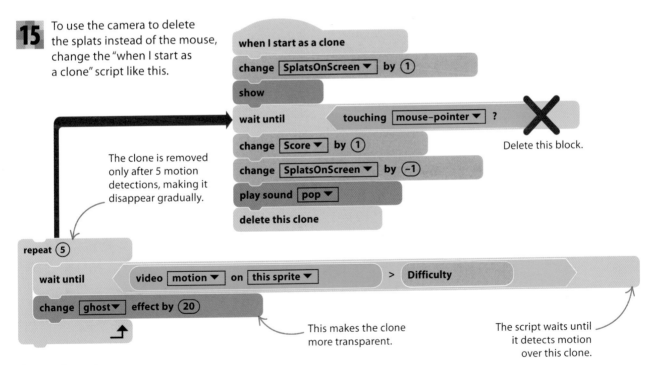

The clone is removed only after 5 motion detections, making it disappear gradually.

Delete this block.

This makes the clone more transparent.

The script waits until it detects motion over this clone.

△ **How it works**
The old script just waited for the mouse-pointer to touch the splat clone before removing it. Now we wait for the webcam to detect motion in the area touching the clone, but we do this five times, increasing the ghost effect each time so the clone gets fainter. So as you rub the splat, it becomes transparent and then disappears.

16 Run the game. You'll probably get a pop-up asking if Scratch can use your webcam. It's OK to click "Accept". You'll then be able to see yourself behind the splats. Try rubbing some splats out with your hand. If they aren't disappearing, put a lower number in the "set Difficulty" block and rerun the game.

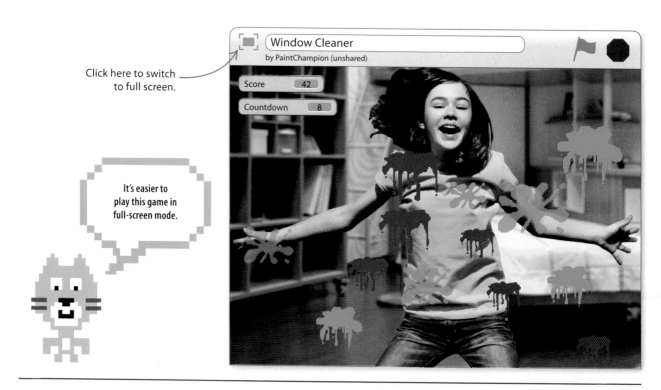

Click here to switch to full screen.

It's easier to play this game in full-screen mode.

Hacks and tweaks

Here are some tips to tweak this game, but feel free to try out your own ideas. Once you know how to use Scratch's motion-detection feature, you can create all sorts of games that encourage players to jump about and have fun!

The "High Score" variable only changes when a player beats it.

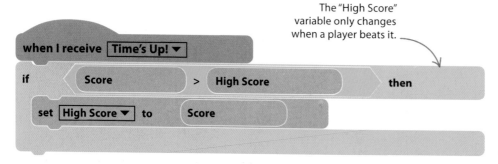

```
when I receive  Time's Up! ▼

if      Score      >    High Score      then

    set  High Score ▼  to    Score
```

◁ **High score**
It's easy to add a high score to the game: just make a new variable, "High Score", and add this script. You could also show the top player's name (see how in the Tunnel of Doom project).

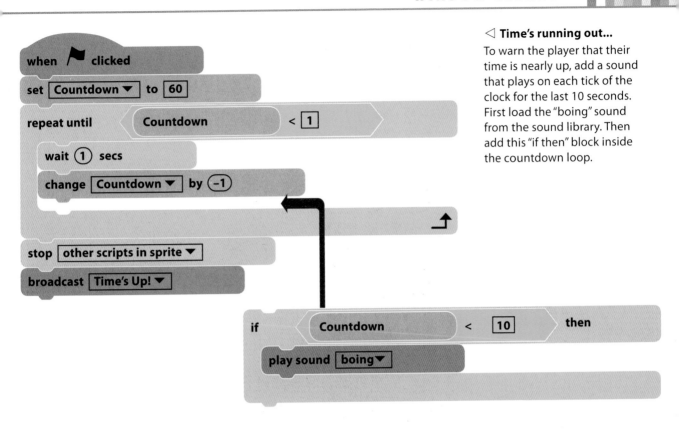

◁ **Time's running out...**

To warn the player that their time is nearly up, add a sound that plays on each tick of the clock for the last 10 seconds. First load the "boing" sound from the sound library. Then add this "if then" block inside the countdown loop.

▽ **Difficulty slider**

If you find you have to change the difficulty setting a lot, you can display it on the stage as a slider. Tick the variable's tick box to make it appear on the stage. Then right-click (or control/shift-click) on it and choose "slider".

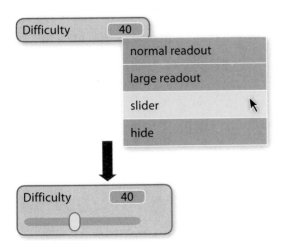

• •   TRY THIS

Multiplayer version

Here's a challenge to test your coding skills. Save a copy of your Window Cleaner game and then try to adapt it to make a multiplayer game in which each player has to rub out splats of a particular colour. You'll need to create score variables for each player, and you'll need to add "if then" blocks to the clones' script to update the different scores depending on which costume has been rubbed out.

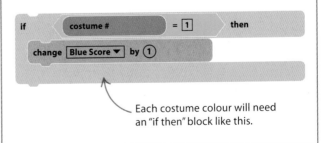

Each costume colour will need an "if then" block like this.

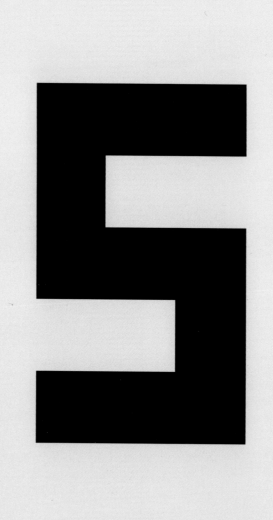

Simulations

Virtual Snow

You don't want real snow inside your computer – it would melt and ruin the circuits. This project shows you how to make perfectly safe virtual snow using Scratch. It falls from the sky and can be made to settle on the ground or stick to things.

How it works

Each snowflake is a clone that moves down the stage from top to bottom, jiggling from side to side like a real snowflake. When the snowflake lands on something or hits the bottom, it stamps an image of itself.

The snowflakes are clones of a simple circle shape.

Snow falls from the top and settles at the bottom.

The snow piles up on the sprite.

△ **Snowman**
In this project, you can load any sprite and make snow stick to it. The snowman and tree sprites work well.

△ **Hidden pictures**
You can add invisible objects that slowly reveal themselves as the snow sticks to them. Use a sprite from the library, draw your own object, or write your name in huge letters.

Let it snow

Start off by drawing the snowflake costume, which is simply a white circle. Then make it snow by creating clones – each one a tiny snowflake falling from the top to the bottom of the stage.

1 Start a new project. Delete the cat sprite and click on the paint symbol ✏ in the sprites list to make a new sprite with the paint editor. Before you start painting, click on the "i" symbol and rename the sprite "Snowflake".

Click to open the information panel.

Type "Snowflake" here.

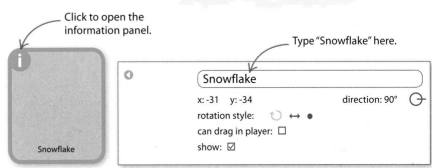

Snowflake

x: -31   y: -34   direction: 90°
rotation style:
can drag in player: ☐
show: ☑

Snowflake

2 In the paint editor, choose the ellipse tool and draw a small white circle in the middle. Hold down the shift key as you draw the circle to make sure it isn't oval-shaped.

Ellipse tool

Select white.

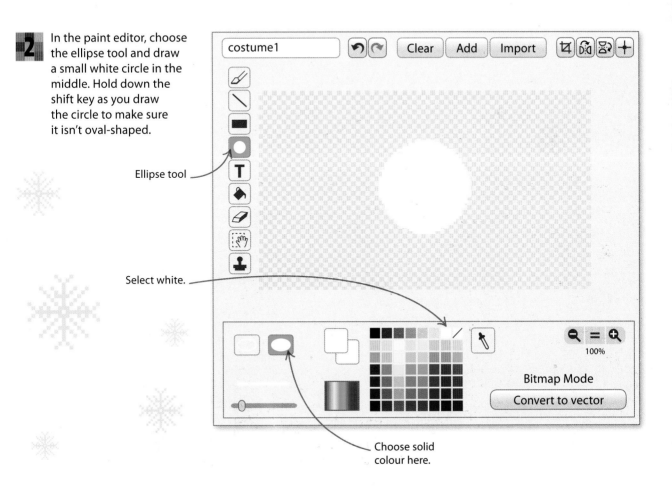

Choose solid colour here.

3 To make sure the circle is the right size, draw a box around it with the select tool and drag one of the box's corners to resize the circle. Aim for a size of 50x50. Centre the costume by selecting the centre tool and clicking in the centre of the circle.

Centre tool

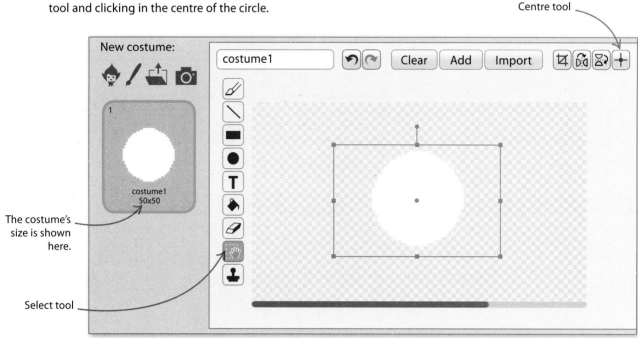

The costume's size is shown here.

Select tool

4 Now add a background so that you can see the falling snow. Click on the paint symbol / in the lower left of Scratch to create a new backdrop in the paint editor.

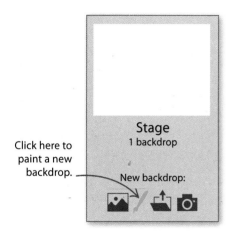

Click here to paint a new backdrop.

5 To make things more interesting, you can use a blend of two colours to fill the background. Choose the darkest blue in the colour palette as your first stored colour. Then choose a paler blue as your second stored colour.

You can store two selected colours at once in the colour palette. Click here to switch to your second selected colour.

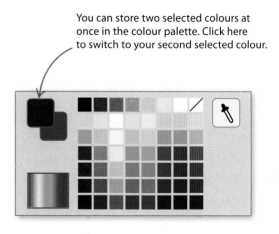

6 Now select the fill tool and choose the vertical gradient option in the lower left. Click in the backdrop to fill it. You can use any colours you like, but snow shows up better on dark colours.

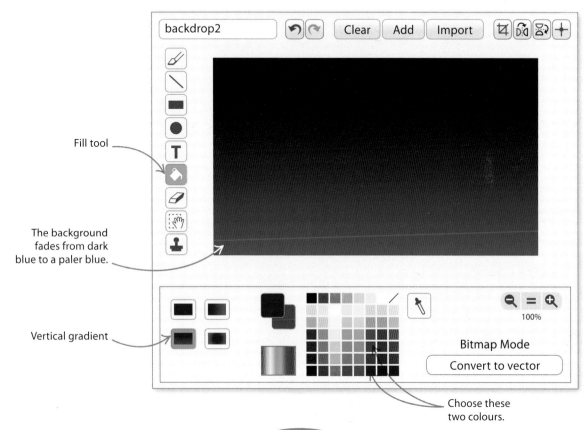

Fill tool

The background fades from dark blue to a paler blue.

Vertical gradient

Choose these two colours.

7 Select the snowflake from the sprites list and open the Scripts tab. Add this script to make clones of the snowflake. Don't run the project yet.

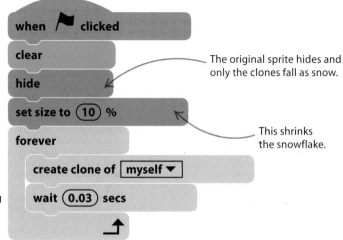

when 🏳 clicked
clear
hide
set size to (10) %
forever
　create clone of | myself ▼
　wait (0.03) secs

The original sprite hides and only the clones fall as snow.

This shrinks the snowflake.

8 Now add a script to make the cloned snowflakes fall from the top of the stage to the bottom, jiggling as they go.

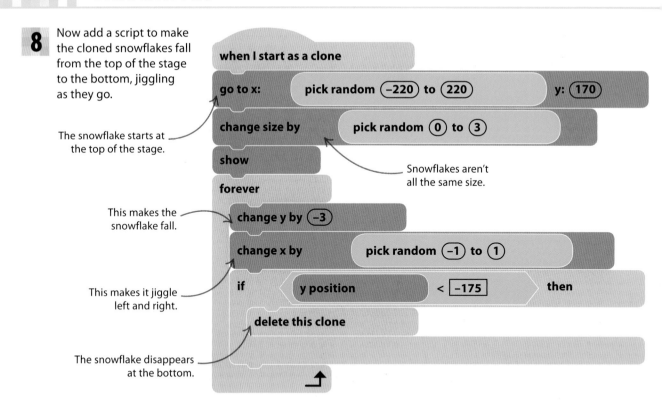

The snowflake starts at the top of the stage.

```
when I start as a clone
go to x: pick random (-220) to (220)    y: (170)
change size by    pick random (0) to (3)
show
forever
    change y by (-3)
    change x by    pick random (-1) to (1)
    if    y position    < -175    then
        delete this clone
```

Snowflakes aren't all the same size.

This makes the snowflake fall.

This makes it jiggle left and right.

The snowflake disappears at the bottom.

9 Run the project. The snow should fall down the stage before disappearing at the bottom.

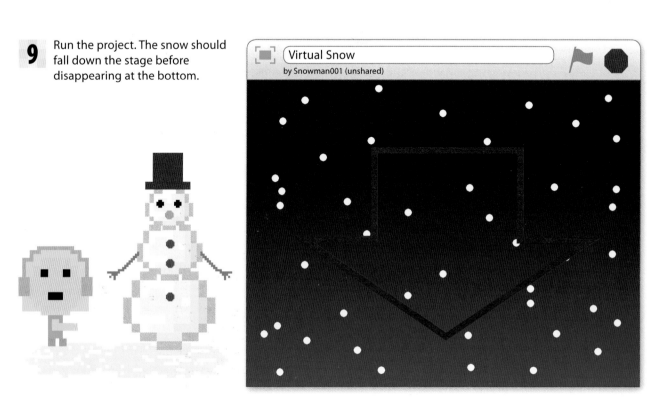

Virtual Snow
by Snowman001 (unshared)

Snowdrifts

In really cold weather, snow doesn't just vanish when it hits the ground – it piles up. It's simple to make your virtual snow settle or stick to other things. Just follow these steps.

10 First to make the snow settle at the bottom. We could just leave the clones there, but Scratch won't let more than 300 clones appear on the stage at once, so you'd run out of snow. An easy fix is to stamp a copy of each clone before deleting it.

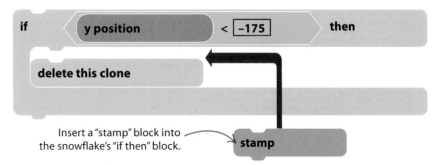

Insert a "stamp" block into the snowflake's "if then" block.

11 Run the project and snow should collect on the floor, but only in a thin layer. To make it build up, add another "if then" block to stamp copies of the clones whenever they touch anything white – such as other snowflakes.

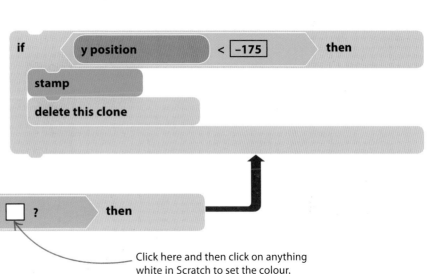

Click here and then click on anything white in Scratch to set the colour.

12 Run the project and watch the snow pile up. You'll notice a problem. The snowflakes are building up in beautiful sculptures rather than settling in a blanket, as real snow does.

Snowflakes stick to anything white.

There's no business like snow business!

13 To make the snow settle in a thick blanket, try this change to the code. Now when a snowflake touches something white, it rolls a dice – only if it gets a 1 does it stick. This makes the snow less sticky and more likely to travel further and build a solid layer.

Add an "and" block to check both conditions are true.

This block is true when Scratch rolls a 1.

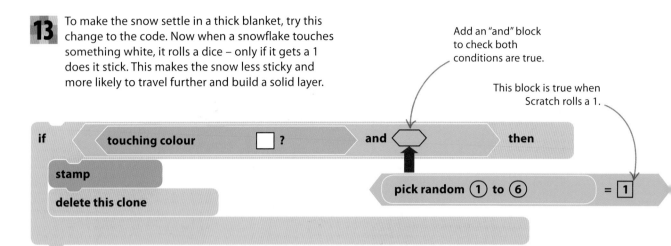

if touching colour ☐ ? and ⬡ then

stamp

delete this clone

pick random ① to ⑥ = 1

14 Run the project to see what happens. You can experiment with changing the 6 in the random block to other numbers. The bigger the number, the flatter the settled snow.

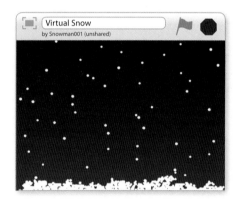

Virtual Snow
by Snowman001 (unshared)

15 Now add a sprite for the snow to fall on. Click the sprite symbol ♦ in the sprites list and choose something from the library, such as the snowman. Add a new "if then" block to the script, as shown here, to make the snow stick to your sprite.

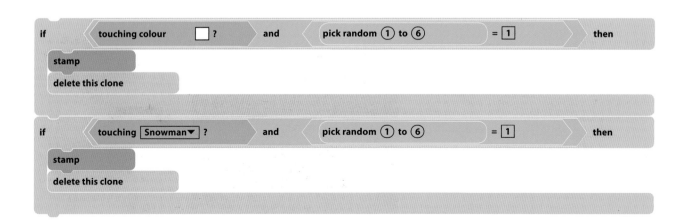

if touching colour ☐ ? and pick random ① to ⑥ = 1 then

stamp

delete this clone

if touching [Snowman▼] ? and pick random ① to ⑥ = 1 then

stamp

delete this clone

Turbo Mode

If you're impatient to see the snow building up, you can speed things up by putting Scratch in "Turbo Mode". Hold down shift and click on the green flag before you run the project. Scratch then runs the scripts much more quickly, with minimum time between blocks. Your snowdrift will now pile up much faster.

Shift-click the green flag to switch Turbo Mode on and off.

Secret pictures

It's easy to modify this project so that the snow sticks to an invisible object, slowly revealing it. Save your project as a copy before you try doing this.

16 Click on the paint symbol ✏ in the sprites list to create a new sprite. Click the blue "i" and name it "Invisible". Now use the paint editor to create your hidden object. It can be anything – a house, an animal, or someone's name – but make it big and use only one colour. You can give the sprite more than one costume if you like.

17 Add this script to the invisible sprite to position and hide it using the ghost effect. Using a "hide" block wouldn't work because that would stop snow sticking to it.

This hides the sprite but allows snowflake clones to detect it.

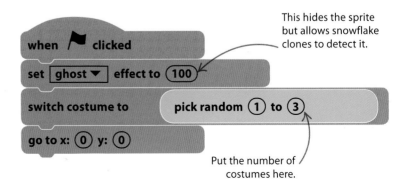

```
when 🏳 clicked

set ghost ▼ effect to 100

switch costume to    pick random 1 to 3

go to x: 0 y: 0
```

Put the number of costumes here.

18 Change the clone script to look like this. Now the snowflakes will only settle on the invisible sprite. They just disappear if they reach the bottom of the stage.

Another snowy day!
My favourite!

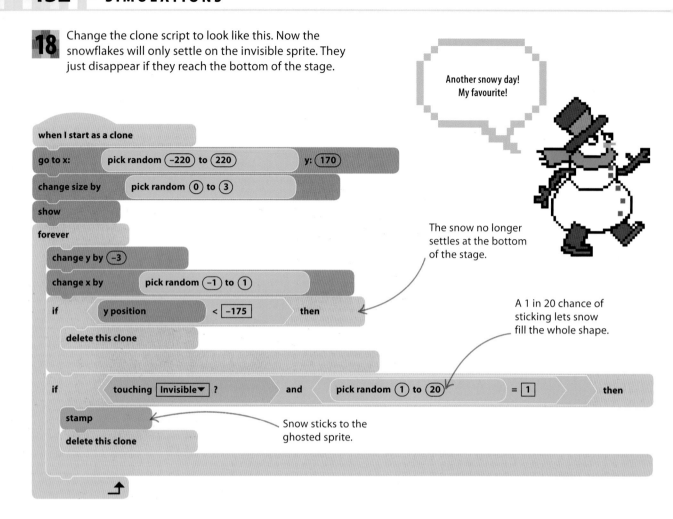

```
when I start as a clone
go to x: pick random (-220) to (220)   y: (170)
change size by   pick random (0) to (3)
show
forever
    change y by (-3)
    change x by   pick random (-1) to (1)
    if   y position   < -175   then
        delete this clone

    if   touching Invisible▼ ?   and   pick random (1) to (20)   = 1   then
        stamp
        delete this clone
```

The snow no longer settles at the bottom of the stage.

A 1 in 20 chance of sticking lets snow fill the whole shape.

Snow sticks to the ghosted sprite.

19 Next add a cool backdrop like "winter-lights" from the library and watch your hidden shape appear in the snow. You can remove the "wait" block from the clone-making loop or use Turbo Mode to speed things up.

Hacks and tweaks

Falling snow or rain can make a great addition to any project or game. Try these hacks to send a snowstorm through your whole Scratch collection!

▷ **Sticky snowballs**
Occasionally, you might see clumps of snow just hanging in the sky. This starts when two snowflakes touch each other as they fall and stamp themselves in the sky. Once there, the clump grows as more snowflakes stick to it. If you follow the instructions in this project carefully it shouldn't happen too often, but if it does, try experimenting with the numbers in the scripts. You can change the size and speed of the snowflakes, the amount they jiggle, and the delay between making each clone.

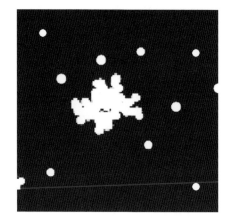

TRY THIS

Starship

If you change the snowflake into a white or yellow dot and remove the random "change x" block that jiggles the falling snow, you get a starfield moving from the top to the bottom of the stage. Add a black backdrop, a spaceship, and some asteroids and you've made a simple rocket game.

▽ **Adding snow to a project**
You can use the falling snow scripts from steps 1–8 to add snow to another project – a great addition to a project like a Christmas card. The snow doesn't sense other sprites so is just a special effect. You'll need to add a "go to front" block to the start of the clone script to make the snowflakes fall in front of other sprites. Change the snowflake to a dark grey raindrop if you want to make it rain.

Add this block to the start of the existing script.

```
when I start as a clone
            go to front
go to x:   pick random (-220) to (220)          y: (170)
```

Firework Display

You might think you'd need lots of sprites to create a firework display, but Scratch's clones feature makes it easy. Clones are great for making explosions and other moving patterns. Computer graphics created with this technique are known as "particle effects".

How it works

Click anywhere on the stage to make a rocket shoot up to that point and explode into a colourful firework. Each firework consists of hundreds of clones of a single sprite. The project uses simulated gravity to make the clones fall as they fly outwards, while flickering or fading.

◁ **Rocket**
Each firework starts off as a rocket launched at the click of a mouse. You can use a simple coloured line to represent the rocket or create a more detailed one in Scratch's paint editor.

◁ **Clones**
To create the globes of coloured "stars", this project uses 300 clones, the maximum number that Scratch allows. Each clone follows a slightly different path at a slightly different speed to make the stars spread out in a circle.

Click this icon to make the project fill your screen.

The rocket shoots upwards before each firework explodes.

Firework Display
by MagicLight01 (unshared)

The stage flashes white at the moment of detonation.

Each explosion is made up of hundreds of clones that spread out from the rocket.

Find out how to add curving trails in the Hacks and Tweaks section.

You can create your own backdrop for the firework display.

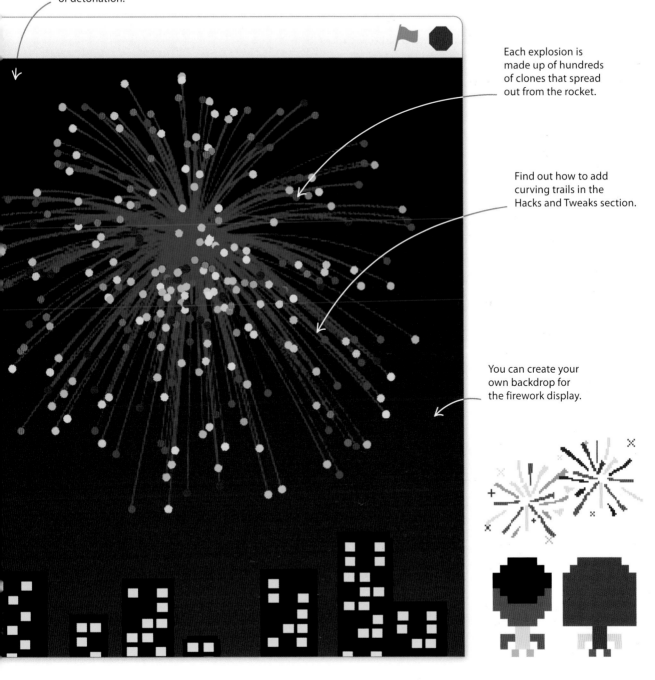

Creating the rocket

The first step in the project is to create the small rocket that shoots up into the sky and explodes in a blaze of fireworks. The script will make the rocket fly to wherever you click the mouse-pointer.

1 Start a new project and delete the cat sprite by right-clicking on it and then selecting "delete". Click on the paint symbol / in the sprites list to create a new sprite and open the paint editor. Rename the sprite "Rocket".

New sprite: 👤 / 📤 📷

2 Use the line and brush tools to paint a rocket firework. A simple red line will do the job as the rocket will be small, but you can make it more realistic if you like.

We have ignition!

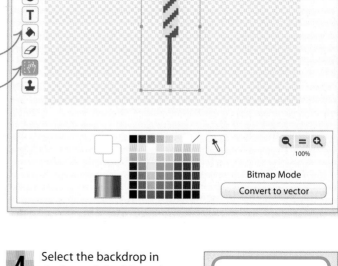

Brush tool
Line tool
Fill tool
Select tool
Centre tool

costume1 | Clear | Add | Import

Bitmap Mode
Convert to vector

100%

3 When you're happy with the firework, use the select tool to drag a box around it. Then grab one of the corners and shrink the costume until it's no wider than 10 and no taller than 50. You can see the size in the costume list. Then centre the sprite using the centre tool.

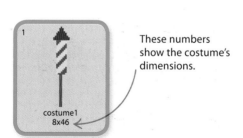

These numbers show the costume's dimensions.

costume1
8x46

4 Select the backdrop in the lower left of Scratch and open the Backdrops tab. Change the name of "backdrop1" to "Flash". This will provide a flash of light when a firework goes off. Click the paint symbol / under the words "New backdrop" to create the main backdrop and call it "Night".

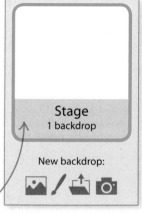

Stage
1 backdrop

New backdrop:
🖼️ / 📤 📷

Click here to select the backdrop.

5 To make the night background more interesting, you can use two colours to create a gradient rather than filling it with solid black. Select the fill tool and choose the two darkest blues in the colour selector. Then click the lower-left gradient tool. Use the fill tool to paint the background so it's dark at the top but pale at the bottom. For extra decoration, add black and yellow rectangles to create a city skyline.

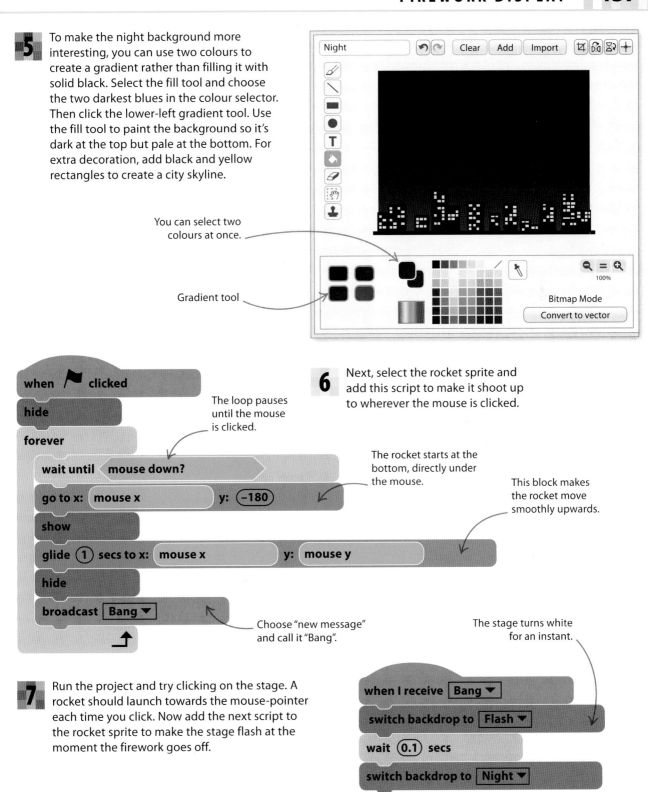

You can select two colours at once.

Gradient tool

Night | Clear | Add | Import

Bitmap Mode
Convert to vector

6 Next, select the rocket sprite and add this script to make it shoot up to wherever the mouse is clicked.

when ⚑ clicked
hide
forever
 wait until ⟨ mouse down? ⟩
 go to x: (mouse x) y: (-180)
 show
 glide (1) secs to x: (mouse x) y: (mouse y)
 hide
 broadcast [Bang ▼]

The loop pauses until the mouse is clicked.

The rocket starts at the bottom, directly under the mouse.

This block makes the rocket move smoothly upwards.

Choose "new message" and call it "Bang".

7 Run the project and try clicking on the stage. A rocket should launch towards the mouse-pointer each time you click. Now add the next script to the rocket sprite to make the stage flash at the moment the firework goes off.

The stage turns white for an instant.

when I receive [Bang ▼]
switch backdrop to [Flash ▼]
wait (0.1) secs
switch backdrop to [Night ▼]

Exploding stars

Real fireworks are packed with hundreds of "stars" – flammable pellets that glow with dazzling colours as they fly apart and burn. You can simulate the appearance of firework stars by using Scratch's clones feature. Follow the instructions here to create the stars and make them explode.

8 Click the paint symbol **/** in the sprites list to create a new sprite and call it "Stars". Before drawing it, select "Convert to vector" in the bottom right of the paint editor, as using vector graphics will help keep the stars circular even when they are very small.

9 Click the plus sign to zoom in to 1600 per cent as the costume will be very small. A simple green circle is all you need to create a star. Choose bright green in the colour palette, select the circle tool, and then choose the solid colour option in the bottom left. To draw a circle, hold down the shift key on the keyboard as you drag. To make sure the costume is centred, select the centre tool and click in the middle of it.

Aim for a size of 5x5.

Choose the solid colour option.

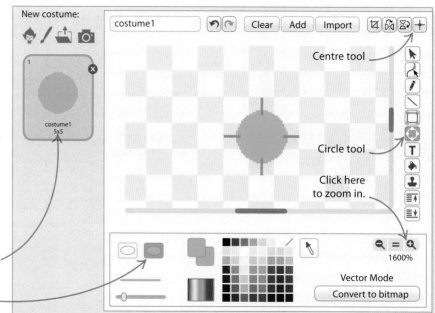

Centre tool

Circle tool

Click here to zoom in.

10 Look in the costume list to check the circle's size – it needs to be about 5x5. If it's too large or small, choose the select tool **▶** and click on the green circle to make a box appear around it. Click on one of the corners and drag it to change the size. Re-centre the costume when you're done.

costume1
5x5

11 Now add the following script to the stars sprite to create 300 hidden copies that will form the explosion.

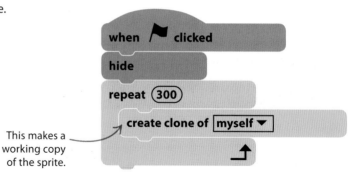

This makes a working copy of the sprite.

12 Click on Data in the blocks palette and make a new variable called "speed". Choose "for this sprite only" in the dialogue box. This allows each clone to have its own copy of the variable with its own value, which makes each star unique. Uncheck the variable's tick box so it doesn't appear on the stage.

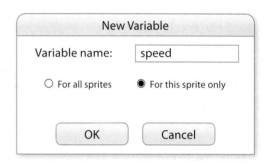

New Variable

Variable name: speed

○ For all sprites ● For this sprite only

OK   Cancel

13 Next, add this script to the stars sprite to create an explosion. Every clone will run its own copy of this script.

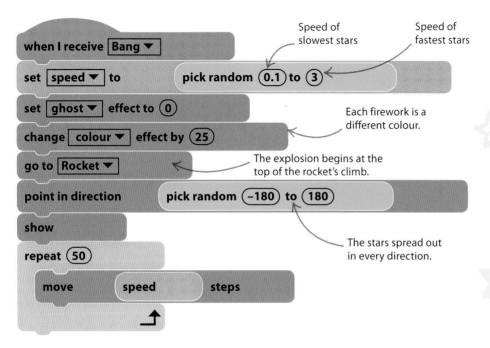

when I receive Bang ▼

set speed ▼ to pick random 0.1 to 3

Speed of slowest stars

Speed of fastest stars

set ghost ▼ effect to 0

change colour ▼ effect by 25

Each firework is a different colour.

go to Rocket ▼

The explosion begins at the top of the rocket's climb.

point in direction pick random -180 to 180

The stars spread out in every direction.

show

repeat 50

move speed steps

14 Add this second "repeat" loop to the bottom of the script to make the stars slow down, fade away, and then disappear.

This block reduces the stars' speed a little with each repeat.

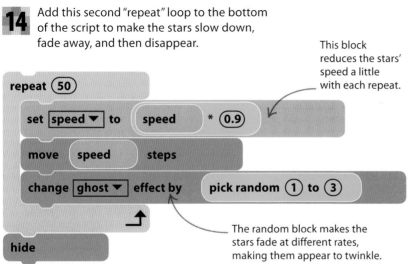

repeat 50

set speed ▼ to speed * 0.9

move speed steps

change ghost ▼ effect by pick random 1 to 3

The random block makes the stars fade at different rates, making them appear to twinkle.

hide

15 Try running the project. When the rocket explodes, you should see hundreds of colourful stars fly outwards before fading.

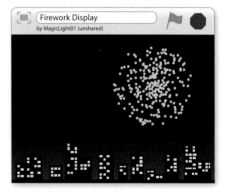

Firework Display
by MagicLight01 (unshared)

Hacks and tweaks

Try some of these changes to create new types of firework with multiple colours or trails. You can also use clones to create many other visual effects – or "particle effects", as computer artists call them.

▽ Sticky stars

You might sometimes see a trail of stars in a line if you send up a rocket straight after running the project. This happens if the stars explode before all the clones are created. To fix the bug, add a "broadcast" block to the bottom of the "when flag clicked" script in the stars sprite and change the rocket's script to run only after it receives the message.

Stars sprite

```
when 🏳 clicked
hide
repeat (300)
    create a clone of [myself ▼]
broadcast [Ready ▼]
```

Rocket sprite

```
when I receive [Ready ▼]
forever
    wait until         mouse down?
    go to x:    mouse x        y: (-180)
    show
    glide (1) secs to x:    mouse x    y:    mouse y
    hide
    broadcast [Bang ▼]
```

```
when 🏳 clicked
hide        ✗
```

▽ Changing colours

Firework-makers use chemicals to create different colours. Try this hack to the stars sprite to make the colours change as the firework explodes.

The colours change as the firework expands.

```
when I receive [Bang ▼]
repeat (100)
    change [colour ▼] effect by (2)
```

Increase the number to see the colours change more quickly.

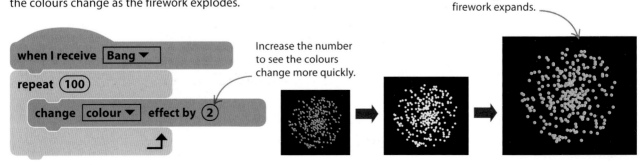

▽ **Multicoloured fireworks**

Try the next hack to give each firework stars with lots of different colours.

When the message is received, every clone runs its own copy of this script.

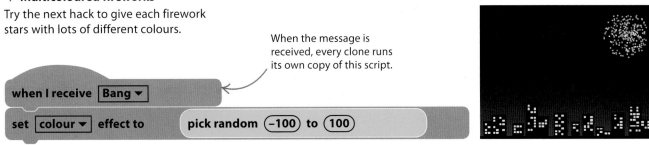

```
when I receive  Bang ▼
set  colour ▼  effect to    pick random ( -100 ) to ( 100 )
```

▷ **Gravity trails**

To make the stars arc downwards under the pull of gravity, leaving colourful trails in their wake, rebuild the script as shown here. Remember to delete the original script when you've finished. As the timer increases, the stars fall more quickly, which is how gravity really works. See if you can figure out how to change the colour of the trails or make them brighten or fade out (hint: you'll need to use the "set pen colour" and "set pen shade" blocks).

This sets the timer to zero. It then counts up in seconds.

The stars fall at an ever greater speed as the timer counts up.

This deletes the trails.

The pen creates the trails.

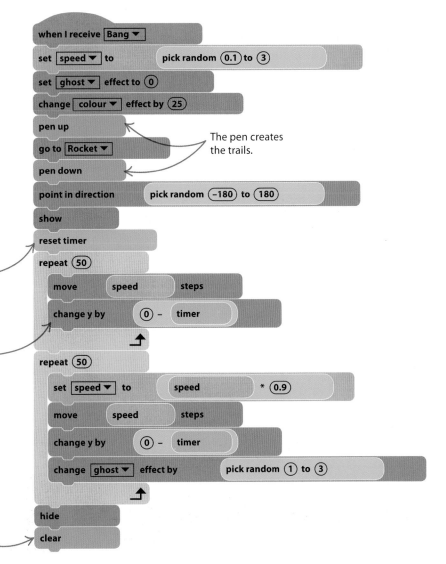

```
when I receive  Bang ▼
set  speed ▼  to    pick random ( 0.1 ) to ( 3 )
set  ghost ▼  effect to ( 0 )
change  colour ▼  effect by ( 25 )
pen up
go to  Rocket ▼
pen down
point in direction    pick random ( -180 ) to ( 180 )
show
reset timer
repeat ( 50 )
    move    speed    steps
    change y by  ( 0 ) –  timer
repeat ( 50 )
    set  speed ▼  to    speed  * ( 0.9 )
    move    speed    steps
    change y by  ( 0 ) –  timer
    change  ghost ▼  effect by    pick random ( 1 ) to ( 3 )
hide
clear
```

Fractal Trees

You might think that drawing a tree requires an artistic eye and a lot of fiddly work, but this project does the job automatically. The code creates special shapes called fractals, simulating the way that trees grow in nature.

Click here to make the tree fill your screen.

Fractal Trees
by SkilledGardener (unshared)

How it works

When you run the project, a tree grows in a split second from the ground up. The tree is a fractal – a shape made from a repeating pattern. If you zoom in to just a part of a fractal, it looks similar to the whole shape. This repetition is easily generated in a computer program by using loops.

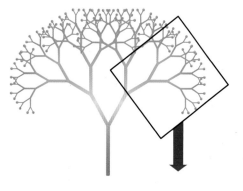

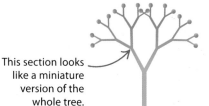

This section looks like a miniature version of the whole tree.

The branches get thinner and greener towards the ends.

Branches are drawn with the Scratch pen.

Each leaf is a clone of the Scratch ball sprite.

A swarm of ball clones draws the tree, doubling in number after each layer of branches.

Romanesco broccoli

Lake Nasser in Egypt

Veins in the human body

△ **Fractals in nature**

Lots of natural objects have fractal shapes, including trees, river systems, clouds, blood vessels, and even broccoli. Natural fractals form most often when something keeps dividing into branches, which is how trees and blood vessels grow.

How it works

In the project Dino Dance Party, we saw how the ballerina's dance routine is based on an algorithm – a set of simple instructions that are followed in strict order. In this project, the code that draws the tree is also based on an algorithm. Try following the three steps below with a pen and paper.

1 Draw a straight line with a thick pen.

2 At the top of each branch draw two shorter, thinner lines at an angle – one to the left and one to the right.

3 Is the tree finished? If the answer is no, go back to step 2. Repeating these simple instructions in a loop creates a complicated pattern with hundreds of branches, just like a real tree.

Leaves and branches

Follow these steps to build a fractal tree, using Scratch's ball sprite for leaves and the Scratch pen to trace branches. The script creates new clones each time a branch divides, making more and more clones as the tree grows from a single trunk to a mass of twigs.

1 Start a new project and delete the cat sprite. Click on the sprite symbol 😺 and add the ball sprite from the library. Rename it "Leaf". Open the Costumes tab and choose the green costume.

Leaf

2 Click on Data and make the following variables for your project: "Angle", "Length", and "ShrinkFactor". Make sure to uncheck their tick boxes so they aren't shown on the stage.

Click here to make each variable.

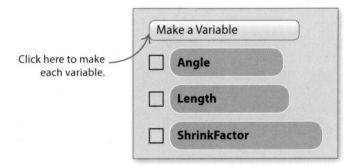

Make a Variable

☐ **Angle**

☐ **Length**

☐ **ShrinkFactor**

3 Add this script to the leaf sprite. You'll need to create the two new messages: "Draw Branch" and "Split Branch". Don't run it yet.

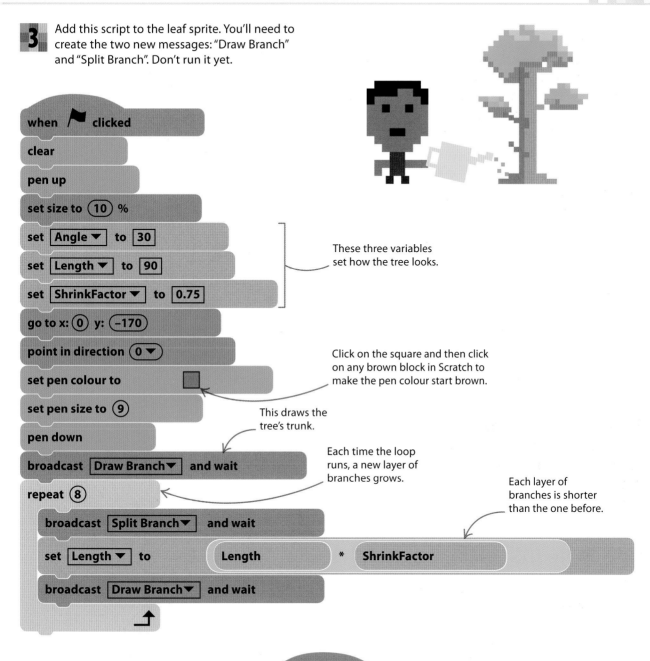

when 🏴 clicked

clear

pen up

set size to (10) %

set [Angle ▼] to [30]

set [Length ▼] to [90]

set [ShrinkFactor ▼] to [0.75]

These three variables set how the tree looks.

go to x: (0) y: (-170)

point in direction (0 ▼)

set pen colour to ■

Click on the square and then click on any brown block in Scratch to make the pen colour start brown.

set pen size to (9)

pen down

This draws the tree's trunk.

broadcast [Draw Branch ▼] and wait

Each time the loop runs, a new layer of branches grows.

repeat (8)

  broadcast [Split Branch ▼] and wait

  Each layer of branches is shorter than the one before.

  set [Length ▼] to (Length * ShrinkFactor)

  broadcast [Draw Branch ▼] and wait

4 Now add this separate script. When it receives the "Draw Branch" message from the main script, it tells every clone to draw a branch and then changes the settings so the next branch will be greener and thinner.

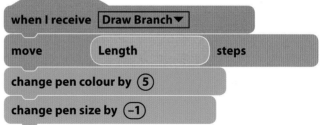

when I receive [Draw Branch ▼]

move (Length) steps

change pen colour by (5)

change pen size by (-1)

5 Add the next script to make the branches divide. It works by cloning each ball, forming a pair, and rotating them to face different directions. Once this script is run, there will be two clones at the end of every branch, each facing a different direction – ready to draw the next two branches.

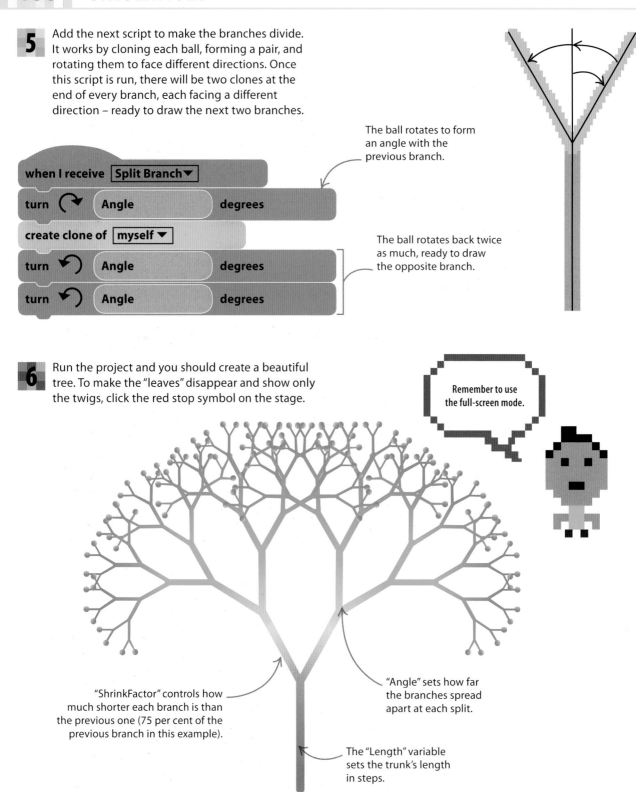

The ball rotates to form an angle with the previous branch.

```
when I receive  Split Branch▼
turn ↻  Angle  degrees
create clone of  myself ▼
turn ↺  Angle  degrees
turn ↺  Angle  degrees
```

The ball rotates back twice as much, ready to draw the opposite branch.

6 Run the project and you should create a beautiful tree. To make the "leaves" disappear and show only the twigs, click the red stop symbol on the stage.

Remember to use the full-screen mode.

"ShrinkFactor" controls how much shorter each branch is than the previous one (75 per cent of the previous branch in this example).

"Angle" sets how far the branches spread apart at each split.

The "Length" variable sets the trunk's length in steps.

7 To make your tree stand out better, try changing the backdrop colour.

Grow a forest

You can adapt this project to grow trees wherever you click, covering the stage with a forest. Make the following changes to the script to do this.

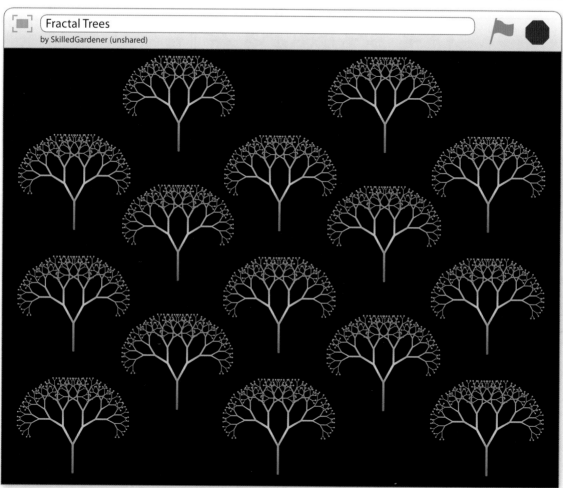

Fractal Trees
by SkilledGardener (unshared)

Open the menu and create a new message called "Kill All Clones".

1 Add this script to stamp the leaves onto the tree before deleting the clones for the next tree.

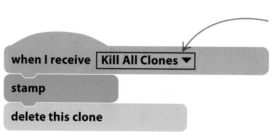

when I receive | Kill All Clones ▼ |

stamp

delete this clone

2 Change the main script to look like this.

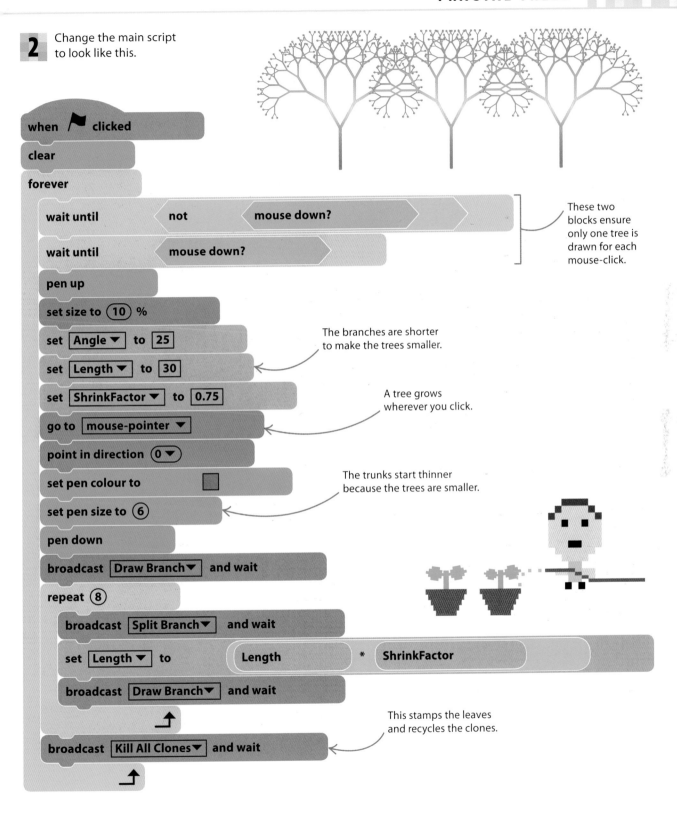

```
when 🏳 clicked
clear
forever
    wait until      not      mouse down?
    wait until      mouse down?
    pen up
    set size to (10) %
    set Angle ▼ to 25
    set Length ▼ to 30
    set ShrinkFactor ▼ to 0.75
    go to mouse-pointer ▼
    point in direction (0 ▼)
    set pen colour to ▢
    set pen size to (6)
    pen down
    broadcast Draw Branch ▼ and wait
    repeat (8)
        broadcast Split Branch ▼ and wait
        set Length ▼ to     Length  *  ShrinkFactor
        broadcast Draw Branch ▼ and wait
    broadcast Kill All Clones ▼ and wait
```

These two blocks ensure only one tree is drawn for each mouse-click.

The branches are shorter to make the trees smaller.

A tree grows wherever you click.

The trunks start thinner because the trees are smaller.

This stamps the leaves and recycles the clones.

Snowflake Simulator

Snowflakes are famous for their amazingly varied shapes – it's said that no two are the same. Even so, all snowflakes share the same underlying structure, with six similar sides. This pattern, known as six-fold symmetry, makes snowflakes easy to mimic on a computer. You can use the same technique used in the Fractal Trees project, but this time every shape will be unique.

Snowflake Simulator
by WhiteSnow2 (unshared)

How it works

When you run this project, a snowflake appears on the stage. Later you can make snowflakes appear wherever you click. Each snowflake is a bit like a fractal tree with six trunks. By using random numbers to set the lengths and angles of the white lines, you can create an endless variety of unique shapes – just like in nature.

△ Real snowflakes

Snowflakes are six-sided because they grow from ice crystals, which are hexagonal. As a snowflake grows, slight changes in air temperature affect the way ice crystals build up. Because every snowflake follows a different path and experiences different changes in temperature, every snowflake is unique.

△ Snow-FAKE

The drawing starts with six versions of the sprite to match the six-fold symmetry of a real snowflake. After that, the lines split in two repeatedly, like the fractal tree, but with more varied angles.

Symmetrical branches

To see how this project uses the ideas from Fractal Trees to make a snowflake, start by following these steps to create a simple, non-random snowflake.

1 Start a new project and delete the cat sprite. Click on the paint symbol / in the sprites list to create a new blank sprite. You don't need to paint a costume because all the drawing will be done by the script.

Sprite1

2 To make the snowflakes show up, paint the backdrop black. Select the backdrop in the lower left of Scratch and click the Backdrops tab above the blocks palette. Then click the fill tool in the paint editor and fill the paint area with black.

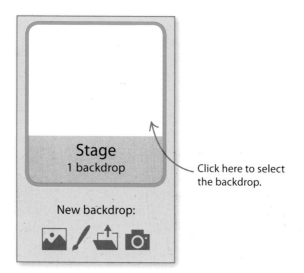

Stage
1 backdrop

Click here to select
the backdrop.

New backdrop:

3 Click on Data in the blocks palette and add five new variables to the project: "Angle", "Length", "Levels", "Symmetry", and "SymmetryAngle". Uncheck their tick boxes so that they don't show on the stage.

Click here to make
each variable.

Sensing

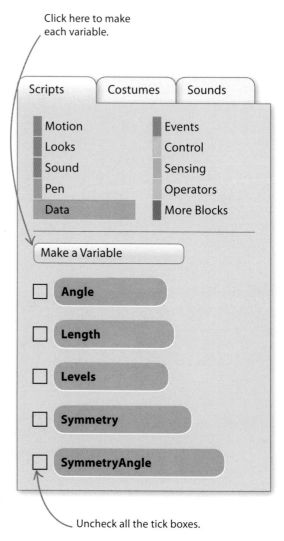

| Scripts | Costumes | Sounds |

Motion   Events
Looks   Control
Sound   Sensing
Pen   Operators
Data   More Blocks

Make a Variable

☐ **Angle**

☐ **Length**

☐ **Levels**

☐ **Symmetry**

☐ **SymmetryAngle**

Uncheck all the tick boxes.

4 Select the sprite in the sprites list and give it the following two scripts. The code creates clones pointing in different directions to make a symmetrical pattern.

The original sprite and the clones all run this script, each drawing an arm in its own direction.

This number sets how many arms the snowflake has.

Open the menu and create a new message called "Draw Level".

```
when ⚑ clicked
set Symmetry ▼ to 6
clear
set pen colour to ☐
set pen size to 1
pen up
go to x: 0 y: 0
pen down
set SymmetryAngle ▼ to    360 / Symmetry
repeat    Symmetry − 1
    create clone of myself ▼
    turn ↻    SymmetryAngle    degrees
set Length ▼ to 100
broadcast Draw Level ▼ and wait
```

```
when I receive Draw Level ▼
move    Length    steps
```

Click on the square here and then on anything white in Scratch.

This calculates the angle between each arm.

The loop adds five clones pointing in different directions.

You can change the number of arms each snowflake has to vary the pattern.

Open the menu and create a new message called "Draw Level".

5 Run the project. Snowflakes need "Symmetry" set to 6, but try other values.

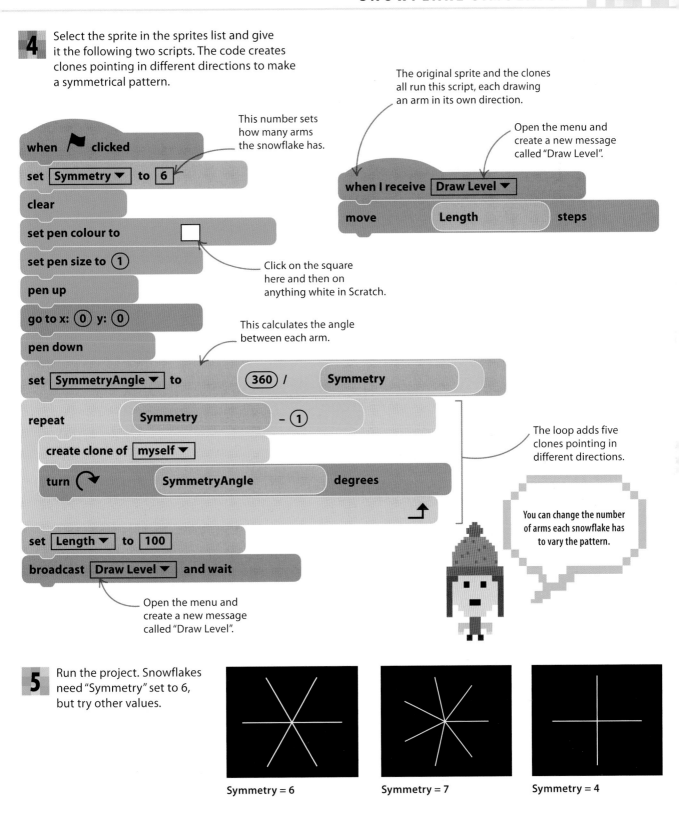

Symmetry = 6   Symmetry = 7   Symmetry = 4

6 To fill in the rest of the snowflake, each clone will draw a succession of branching lines, like a fractal tree. Make the following changes to the main script, but don't run it yet.

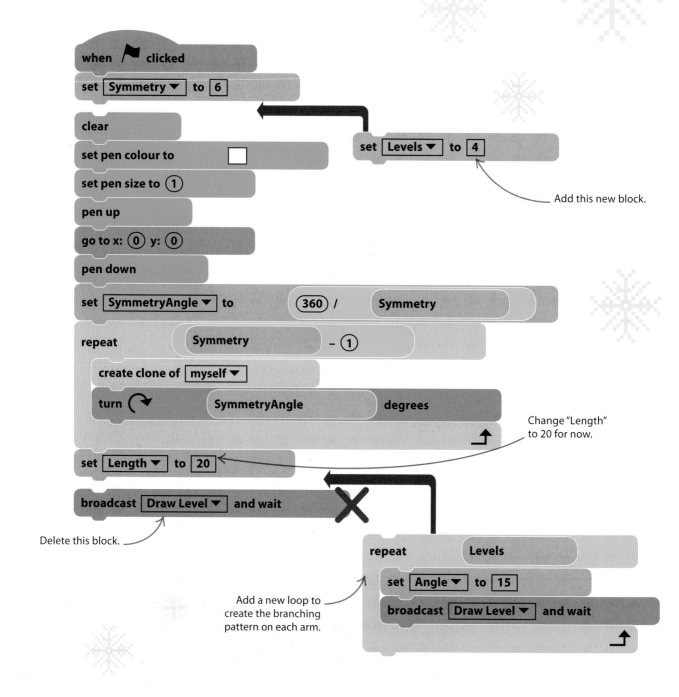

when ⚑ clicked

set Symmetry ▼ to 6

clear

set pen colour to ☐

set pen size to ①

pen up

go to x: ⓪ y: ⓪

pen down

set SymmetryAngle ▼ to (360) / Symmetry

repeat (Symmetry − ①)

　create clone of myself ▼

　turn ↻ (SymmetryAngle) degrees

set Length ▼ to 20

broadcast Draw Level ▼ and wait

set Levels ▼ to 4

Add this new block.

Change "Length" to 20 for now.

Delete this block.

repeat (Levels)

　set Angle ▼ to 15

　broadcast Draw Level ▼ and wait

Add a new loop to create the branching pattern on each arm.

7 Add three new blocks to the "When I receive" script to create new clones. These create a new clone and make the old and new clones face different directions.

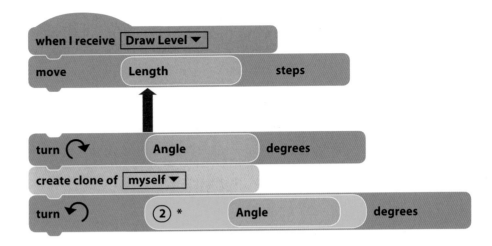

when I receive ｜ Draw Level ▼

move ｜ Length ｜ steps

turn ↻ ｜ Angle ｜ degrees

create clone of ｜ myself ▼

turn ↺ ｜ ② * ｜ Angle ｜ degrees

8 Now run the project. You'll see a branching snowflake like this.

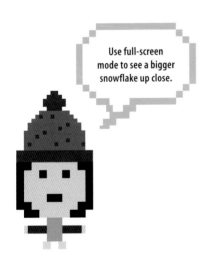

Use full-screen mode to see a bigger snowflake up close.

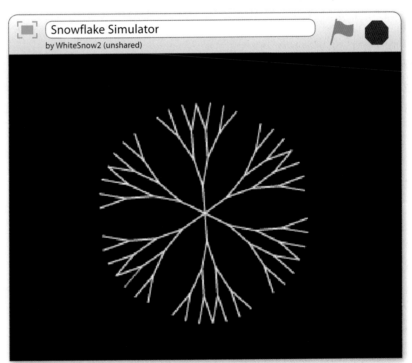

Snowflake Simulator
by WhiteSnow2 (unshared)

9 See what happens when you change the number of "Levels" in the "set" block at the top of the main script.

Levels = 1

Levels = 2

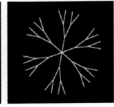

Levels = 3

Levels = 4

10 Now to make each snowflake different. Add some "pick random" blocks to the main script.

Add these new "pick random" blocks.

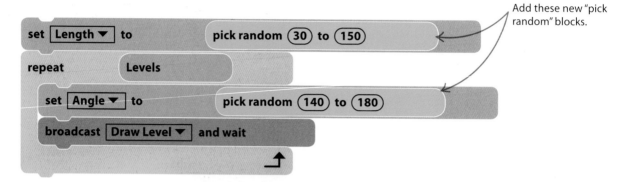

```
set  Length ▼  to          pick random (30) to (150)
repeat              Levels
    set  Angle ▼  to          pick random (140) to (180)
    broadcast  Draw Level ▼  and wait
                                    ↰
```

11 Run the project – you'll get a different snowflake every time.

Hacks and tweaks

Experiment! There are so many numbers to play with in this project, changing any one of them will give very different patterns. Play with the symmetry, levels, angles, and lengths. You can even add colours to your creations.

▷ **Oddflakes**
Try this quick change to make odd-looking snowflakes. It varies the line lengths after each branch point, creating a wider range of flaky weirdness.

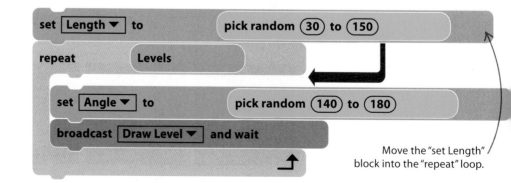

```
set  Length ▼  to          pick random (30) to (150)
repeat              Levels
    set  Angle ▼  to          pick random (140) to (180)
    broadcast  Draw Level ▼  and wait
                                    ↰
```

Move the "set Length" block into the "repeat" loop.

▽ **Click-a-flake**

Make snowflakes wherever you click on the stage with these modifications to the code. There's also a script to clear the stage when you press the space-bar in case things get too messy. Make sure you keep the script from step 7.

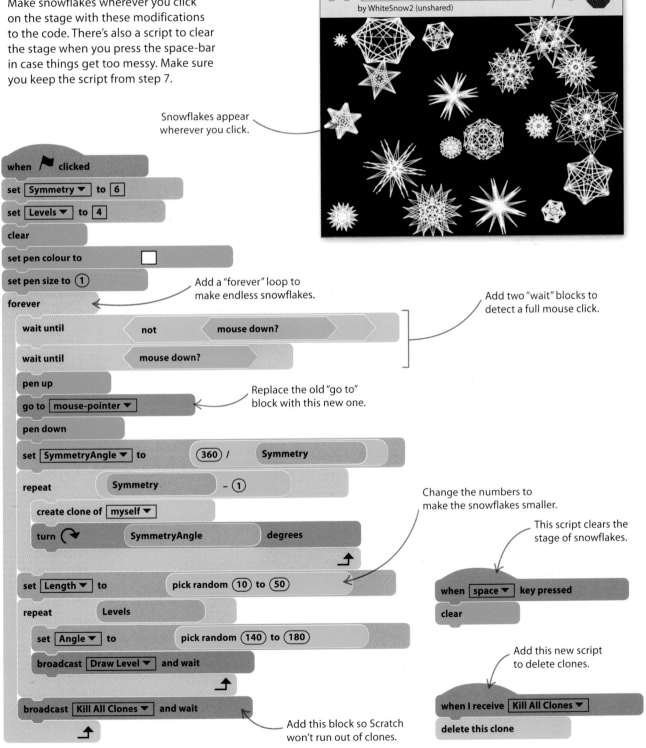

Snowflakes appear wherever you click.

Snowflakes appear wherever you click.

```
when  ⚑  clicked
set  Symmetry ▼  to  6
set  Levels ▼  to  4
clear
set pen colour to  □
set pen size to  ①
forever
    wait until       not       mouse down?
    wait until       mouse down?
    pen up
    go to  mouse-pointer ▼
    pen down
    set  SymmetryAngle ▼  to      360  /    Symmetry
    repeat      Symmetry      – ①
        create clone of  myself ▼
        turn ↻      SymmetryAngle      degrees
    set  Length ▼  to      pick random  10  to  50
    repeat      Levels
        set  Angle ▼  to      pick random  140  to  180
        broadcast  Draw Level ▼  and wait
    broadcast  Kill All Clones ▼  and wait
```

Add a "forever" loop to make endless snowflakes.

Add two "wait" blocks to detect a full mouse click.

Replace the old "go to" block with this new one.

Change the numbers to make the snowflakes smaller.

This script clears the stage of snowflakes.

```
when  space ▼  key pressed
clear
```

Add this new script to delete clones.

```
when I receive  Kill All Clones ▼
delete this clone
```

Add this block so Scratch won't run out of clones.

Music and sound

Sprites and Sounds

Do you have a younger brother or sister who's always trying to play on the computer? Here's something you can create in Scratch to keep them amused. Click on any sprite for a unique action and sound. This project works especially well on a touchscreen computer.

How it works

Sprites and Sounds couldn't be easier to play – simply click the sprites or the background and you'll hear a sound and see an animation or visual effect.

▽ **Virtual circus**
This entertaining project is a mix of funny sounds and moves. You can add as many sprites and sounds as you want to spice up the show.

The project works best in full-screen mode, which stops you from accidentally moving the sprites.

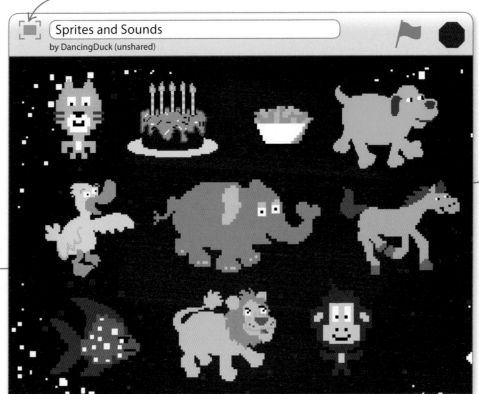

Click anywhere on the stage for some sound and action.

Each sprite performs its own little show when clicked.

Background action

Everything in this project does something interesting when it's clicked, including the background. Follow these steps to create the background, and then start adding sprites.

1 Start a new project. Ignore the cat sprite for now and click on the backdrop symbol 🖼 in the lower left of the Scratch window to open the backdrop library. Load the "sparkling" backdrop.

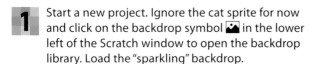

The blue outline shows that the stage is selected.

2 With the stage selected, open the Sounds tab above the blocks palette and then click on the speaker symbol. Choose "fairydust".

This sound is 0.51 seconds long.

3 Now build this script for the stage to create some magic and sparkle when the backdrop is clicked. Check if it works by clicking on the stage.

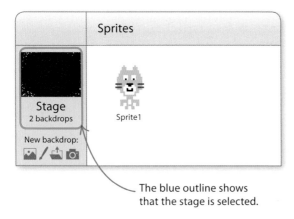

This makes the backdrop flash.

4 Drag the cat sprite to the top-left corner of the stage and add this script.

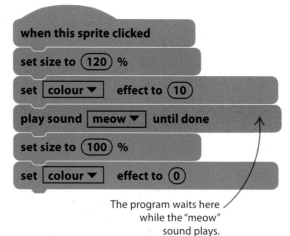

The program waits here while the "meow" sound plays.

5 Click on the cat and see him grow, turn yellow, and meow before returning to normal.

The cat grows in size and changes its colour.

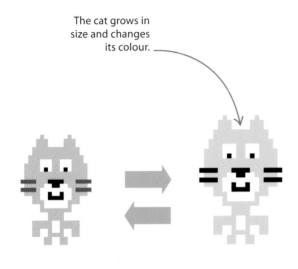

EXPERT TIPS

Sound blocks

There are two versions of the "play sound" block. When you use the short one, the program starts playing the sound but immediately moves on to the next block. This is useful for animations, as it allows you to make a sprite move at the same time as the sound is playing. The longer version of the "play sound" block includes the words "until done". When you use this block, the program waits until the sound has finished before moving on to the next block. This is useful for, say, a costume or size change that should last exactly as long as the sound.

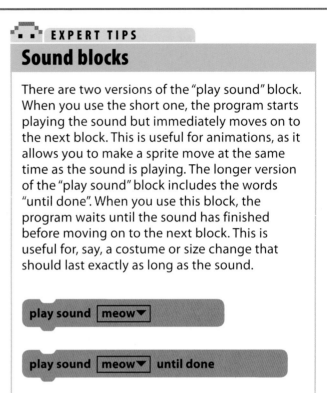

Sprite extravaganza!

Now add the following sprites and their scripts. Some of the sprites have the right sounds built in, but in other cases you'll need to open the Sounds tab and load the sound from Scratch's sound library before you can select it in the script. After building each script, position the sprite on the stage and test it.

6

Duck

Laughing duck

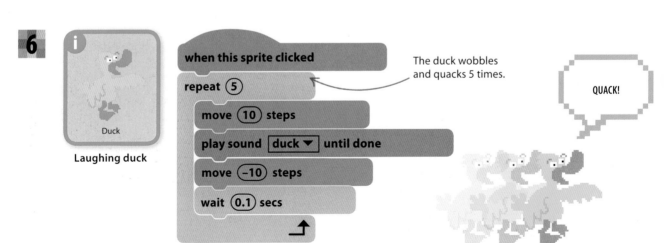

The duck wobbles and quacks 5 times.

QUACK!

7

Cake

Dancing cake

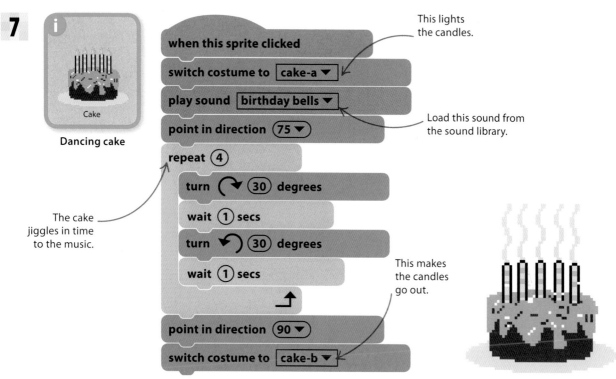

when this sprite clicked

switch costume to [cake-a ▼] — This lights the candles.

play sound [birthday bells ▼] — Load this sound from the sound library.

point in direction (75 ▼)

repeat (4)

The cake jiggles in time to the music. →

    turn ↻ (30) degrees

    wait (1) secs

    turn ↺ (30) degrees

    wait (1) secs

point in direction (90 ▼)

switch costume to [cake-b ▼] — This makes the candles go out.

8

Elephant

Elephant fanfare

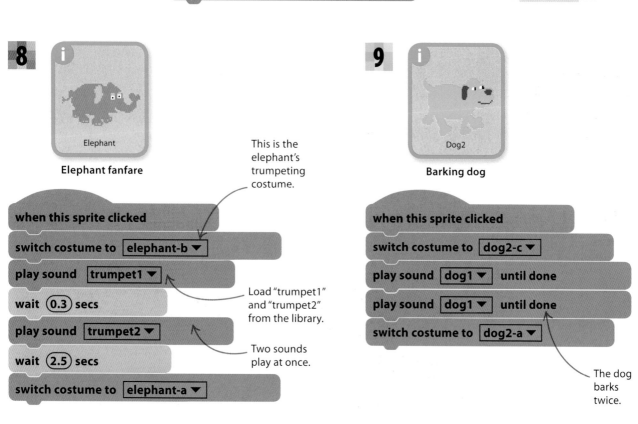

when this sprite clicked

switch costume to [elephant-b ▼] — This is the elephant's trumpeting costume.

play sound [trumpet1 ▼]

wait (0.3) secs

play sound [trumpet2 ▼] — Load "trumpet1" and "trumpet2" from the library.

wait (2.5) secs — Two sounds play at once.

switch costume to [elephant-a ▼]

9

Dog2

Barking dog

when this sprite clicked

switch costume to [dog2-c ▼]

play sound [dog1 ▼] until done

play sound [dog1 ▼] until done

switch costume to [dog2-a ▼] — The dog barks twice.

10

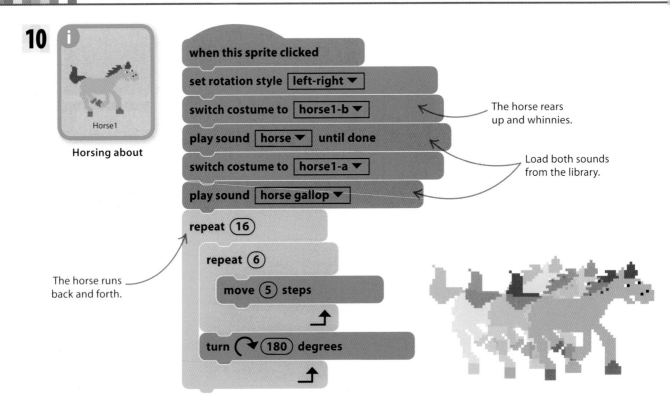

Horse1

Horsing about

```
when this sprite clicked
set rotation style  left-right ▼
switch costume to  horse1-b ▼
play sound  horse ▼  until done
switch costume to  horse1-a ▼
play sound  horse gallop ▼
repeat  16
    repeat  6
        move  5  steps
    turn ↻  180  degrees
```

The horse rears up and whinnies.

Load both sounds from the library.

The horse runs back and forth.

11

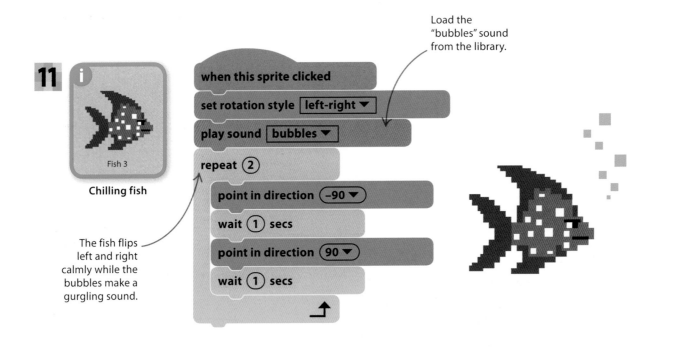

Fish 3

Chilling fish

```
when this sprite clicked
set rotation style  left-right ▼
play sound  bubbles ▼
repeat  2
    point in direction  -90 ▼
    wait  1  secs
    point in direction  90 ▼
    wait  1  secs
```

Load the "bubbles" sound from the library.

The fish flips left and right calmly while the bubbles make a gurgling sound.

12

Lion

King of the jungle

```
when this sprite clicked
switch costume to  lion-b ▼
play sound  meow2 ▼  until done
switch costume to  lion-a ▼
```

"Meow2" is not a roar, but it's the nearest thing in the library!

13

Monkey2

Jumpy monkey

```
when this sprite clicked
play sound  chee chee ▼
repeat  10
    change y by  10
    wait  0.1  secs
    change y by  −10
    wait  0.1  secs
```

Changing the monkey's y coordinate moves it up or down.

Cheese puffs

The last sprite is a bowl of tasty-looking cheese puffs – when you click on the bowl, the cheese puffs will vanish. There isn't a suitable costume for the empty bowl, but you can create one using Scratch's paint editor. The following steps show you how.

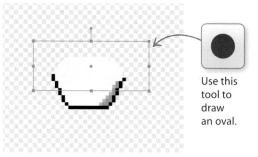

14 Add the Cheesy-Puffs sprite from the library. Then click on the Costumes tab and right-click (or control/shift-click) on the single costume shown and select "duplicate".

15 Select the duplicated costume "cheesy-puffs2". In the paint editor, choose white or cream, and use the ellipse tool to draw an oval over the cheese puffs. Use the eraser tool to get rid of any leftover bits.

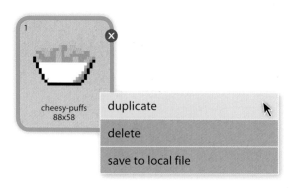

cheesy-puffs
88x58

duplicate
delete
save to local file

Use this tool to draw an oval.

16 Click the Sounds tab above the blocks palette and load the "chomp" sound from the library. Then add the sprite's script.

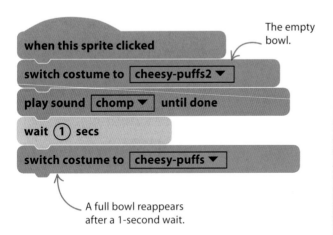

The empty bowl.

```
when this sprite clicked
switch costume to  cheesy-puffs2 ▼
play sound  chomp ▼  until done
wait  1  secs
switch costume to  cheesy-puffs ▼
```

A full bowl reappears after a 1-second wait.

17 Move all your sprites around so they fit nicely on the stage. Then test the project, but remember to click the full-screen symbol first so that the sprites don't accidentally move when you click them. Test every sprite. Note that you don't need to click the green flag to run this project, just click on the sprites.

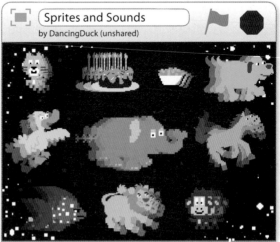

Hacks and tweaks

This project is really a collection of mini-projects – one per sprite. This makes it easy to swap in new sprites or change animations and sounds. Have a look in Scratch's sprite and sound libraries for inspiration. You could also draw your own pictures or record your own sounds.

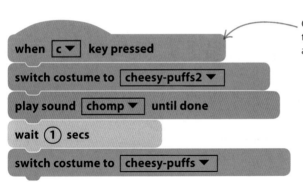

Change the header to trigger the script with a key instead of a click.

```
when  c ▼  key pressed
switch costume to  cheesy-puffs2 ▼
play sound  chomp ▼  until done
wait  1  secs
switch costume to  cheesy-puffs ▼
```

◁ **Animal piano**
For younger children, you could change the scripts so that the animations and sounds are triggered by key presses rather than mouse clicks, turning the computer keyboard into a kind of piano. Choose keys that are widely spread to make the project into a game of "find the key".

▷ Record your own sounds

If your computer has a microphone, then you can give your project a personal touch by recording your own sounds. First select the sprite you want to add a sound to – perhaps the lion, if you want to give him a better roar. Click the Sounds tab and then the microphone symbol 🎤. To start recording, click on the black circle. To stop, click the square.

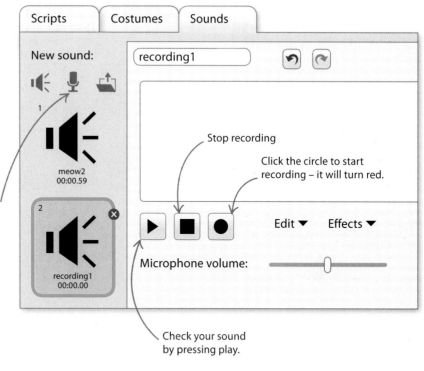

Click here to create a new sound.

Stop recording

Click the circle to start recording – it will turn red.

Check your sound by pressing play.

▷ Editing sounds

Scratch makes it easy to edit sounds that you've recorded or uploaded. Open the Sounds tab and select the sound you want to work on. The black pattern shows the volume of the sound as it plays. Use your mouse to highlight parts of the sound you want to delete or move, and then use the menus below to make changes or add effects.

Highlight parts of the sound you want to edit.

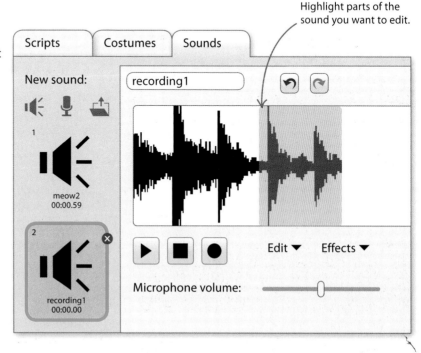

Drumtastic

This project turns your computer keyboard into a drum machine. Type in anything you want and Scratch turns the letters into repeating drum sounds using up to 18 different instruments, from cymbals and bongos to pounding bass drums.

How it works

When you run the project, the Scratch cat asks you to type something in the box. When you press return, the code turns each letter into a different sound and plays the phrase back over and over again. As the sounds play, the coloured drums on the stage flash in time, while the Scratch cat walks to the beat.

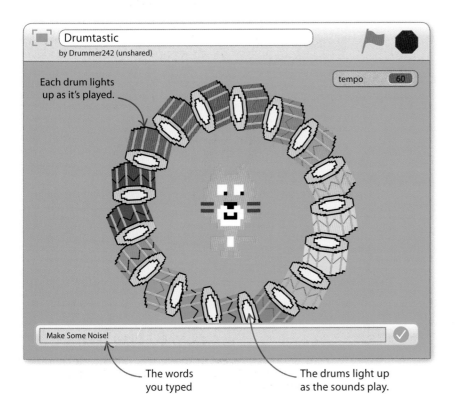

Drumtastic
by Drummer242 (unshared)

tempo 60

Each drum lights up as it's played.

Make Some Noise!

The words you typed

The drums light up as the sounds play.

▽ **Scratch drumkit**
The script turns every letter into a drum sound. There are 26 letters in the alphabet but Scratch only has 18 drum sounds, so some sounds are used for two letters.

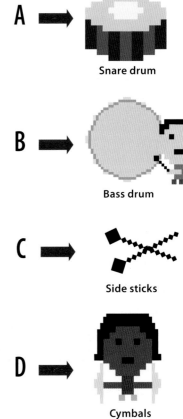

A ➡ Snare drum

B ➡ Bass drum

C ➡ Side sticks

D ➡ Cymbals

Dancing cat

To make the project more fun, the cat will dance and shout out each letter in a speech bubble as the drums play. Follow the steps below to create a custom block that plays the drums and animates the cat.

1 Start a new project and keep the cat sprite. Set the background to a solid colour by clicking the paint symbol / in the lower left of Scratch, picking a cool colour, and using the fill tool ◆ to create a coloured backdrop.

Stage
2 backdrops

New backdrop:

2 Select the cat sprite, click on Data, and add these variables to your project: "Count" and "Words". Leave them ticked so that they show on the stage.

Click here to make each variable.

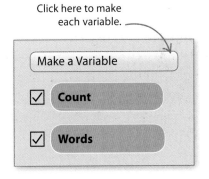

Make a Variable

☑ **Count**

☑ **Words**

3 Now create a custom block for the cat sprite. Choose "More Blocks" in the blocks palette and make a new block called "play a drum". This will trigger a script that plays a drum and makes the cat say the drum's letter at the same time. To keep things simple, the first version of the script will play the same drum sound every time.

Type "play a drum" in here.

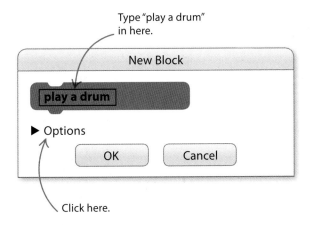

New Block

play a drum

▶ Options

OK   Cancel

Click here.

4 Choose the second option in the menu to add an input window for the drum's letter.

Type the name of the input here: "letter".

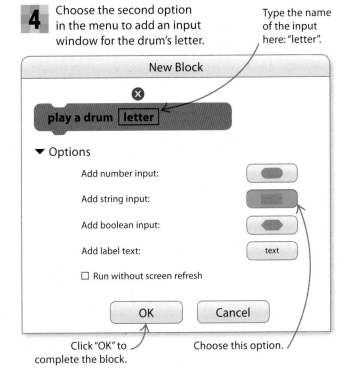

New Block

✕

play a drum letter

▼ Options

Add number input:

Add string input:

Add boolean input:

Add label text: text

☐ Run without screen refresh

OK   Cancel

Click "OK" to complete the block.

Choose this option.

5 Next add this script to the "define play a drum" header block. For now, the cat just says the letter and the script plays only one type of drum: a snare drum. The script will get longer later so that different drums can play.

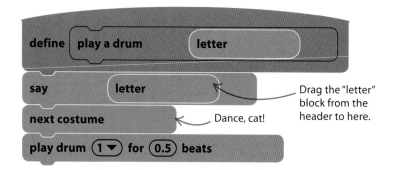

define   play a drum   letter

say   letter

← Drag the "letter" block from the header to here.

next costume   ← Dance, cat!

play drum (1 ▼) for (0.5) beats

LINGO

Strings

Programmers call a sequence of words or letters a string. Think of the letters as being strung together like beads on a necklace.

6 Now add the script below to ask the user to type something on their keyboard. This script sends the letters one at a time to the cat using the "play a drum" block. Anything set as an input in the "play a drum" block is put in the blue "letter" block in the define script.

A, B, C, D, E...

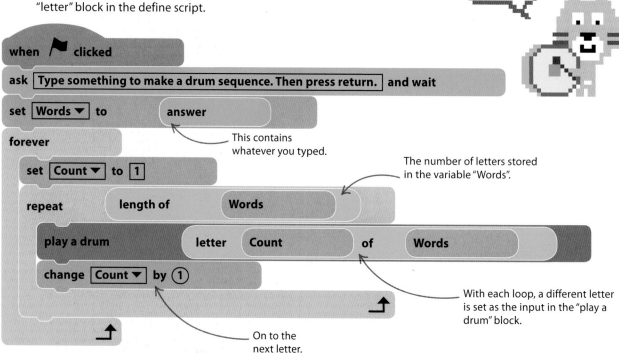

when 🏴 clicked

ask Type something to make a drum sequence. Then press return. and wait

set Words ▼ to   answer

This contains whatever you typed.

forever

set Count ▼ to 1

The number of letters stored in the variable "Words".

repeat   length of   Words

play a drum   letter Count   of   Words

change Count ▼ by ①

With each loop, a different letter is set as the input in the "play a drum" block.

On to the next letter.

7 Run the project. Type "Scratch" and press enter. The cat will shout out the letters of "Scratch" to a drumbeat.

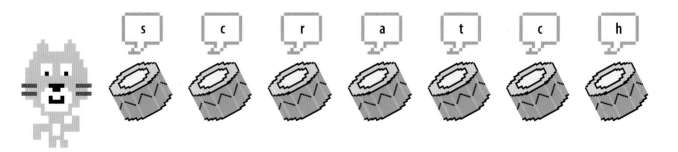

From letters to drums

The next step is to change the code so that each letter plays a particular drum. Scratch has only 18 drum sounds, so some sounds will be played by more than one letter. Spaces and punctuation will create brief pauses in the pattern of drums. Scratch also ignores whether letters are capitals or not – "A" and "a" are treated the same.

Scratch's "play drum" block has 18 built-in sounds.

play drum (1 ▼) for (0.25) beats

(1) Snare Drum	**a, s**
(2) Bass Drum	**b, t**
(3) Side Stick	**c, u**
(4) Crash Cymbal	**d, v**
(5) Open Hi-Hat	**e, w**
(6) Closed Hi-Hat	**f, x**
(7) Tambourine	**g, y**
(8) Hand Clap	**h, z**
(9) Claves	**i**
(10) Wood Block	**j**
(11) Cowbell	**k**
(12) Triangle	**l**
(13) Bongo	**m**
(14) Conga	**n**
(15) Cabasa	**o**
(16) Guiro	**p**
(17) Vibraslap	**q**
(18) Open Cuica	**r**

8 First you need to add four new variables: "Alphabet", which stores the whole alphabet in order; "AlphabetCount", which stores a letter's numerical position in the alphabet from 1 to 26; "NumberOfDrums", for the number of different drum sounds in Scratch; and "ChosenDrum", to hold the number of the drum sound to be played.

Uncheck the tick boxes so the variables don't appear on the stage.

☐ **Alphabet**

☐ **AlphabetCount**

☐ **ChosenDrum**

☐ **NumberOfDrums**

9 Add three new blocks to the start of the main script to set up the "Alphabet" and "NumberOfDrums" variables. The "Draw Drums" message will trigger a script that draws the drums, but that code comes later.

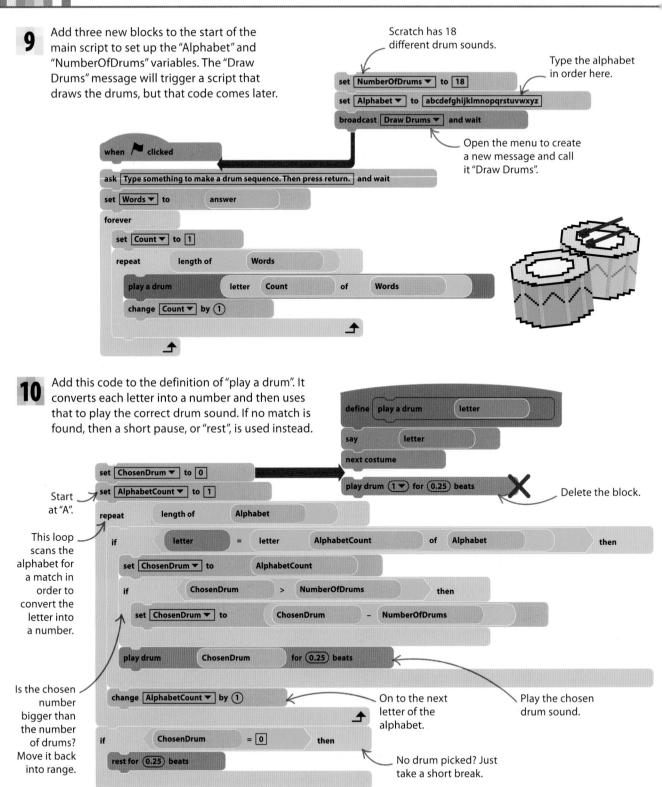

Scratch has 18 different drum sounds.

```
set NumberOfDrums ▼ to 18
set Alphabet ▼ to abcdefghijklmnopqrstuvwxyz
broadcast Draw Drums ▼ and wait
```

Type the alphabet in order here.

Open the menu to create a new message and call it "Draw Drums".

```
when 🏳 clicked
ask Type something to make a drum sequence. Then press return. and wait
set Words ▼ to answer
forever
    set Count ▼ to 1
    repeat    length of    Words
        play a drum    letter    Count    of    Words
        change Count ▼ by 1
```

10 Add this code to the definition of "play a drum". It converts each letter into a number and then uses that to play the correct drum sound. If no match is found, then a short pause, or "rest", is used instead.

```
define play a drum    letter
say    letter
next costume
play drum 1 ▼ for 0.25 beats
```

Delete the block.

```
set ChosenDrum ▼ to 0
set AlphabetCount ▼ to 1
repeat    length of    Alphabet
    if    letter = letter AlphabetCount of Alphabet    then
        set ChosenDrum ▼ to AlphabetCount
        if    ChosenDrum > NumberOfDrums    then
            set ChosenDrum ▼ to ChosenDrum - NumberOfDrums
        play drum ChosenDrum for 0.25 beats
    change AlphabetCount ▼ by 1
if    ChosenDrum = 0    then
    rest for 0.25 beats
```

Start at "A".

This loop scans the alphabet for a match in order to convert the letter into a number.

Is the chosen number bigger than the number of drums? Move it back into range.

On to the next letter of the alphabet.

Play the chosen drum sound.

No drum picked? Just take a short break.

11 Now run the project and see if you can create some cool drumbeats. Try "a a a a abababab", for instance. Remember you can use spaces or punctuation marks to create pauses.

Light-up drums

To make the project look more interesting you can add a circle of 18 coloured drum clones – one for each sound. Each drum will light up when its sound plays.

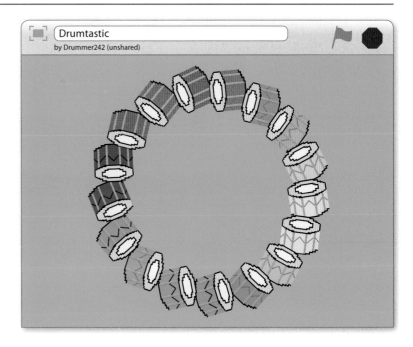

12 Click on the sprite symbol ♠ in the sprites list and add the Drum1 sprite from the library.

13 Add a variable called "drumID", making sure you select "for this sprite only" – this lets every clone have its own copy of the variable. This variable will hold a unique ID number for each drum to help them light up at the right time. Untick this variable so it doesn't show on the stage.

Choose this option or the drums won't work properly.

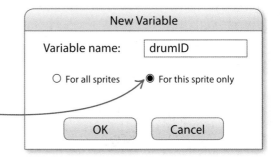

14 Add the script below to the Drum1 sprite. When this script receives the "Draw Drums" message, it draws a ring of coloured drum clones on the stage, each with a unique ID number.

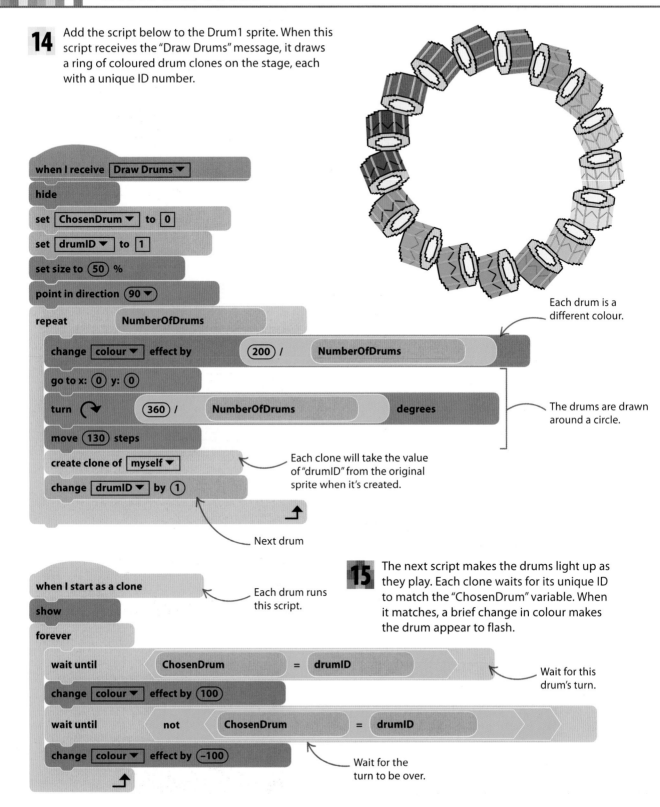

```
when I receive Draw Drums ▼
hide
set ChosenDrum ▼ to 0
set drumID ▼ to 1
set size to 50 %
point in direction 90 ▼
repeat          NumberOfDrums
    change colour ▼ effect by     200 / NumberOfDrums
    go to x: 0 y: 0
    turn ↻     360 / NumberOfDrums     degrees
    move 130 steps
    create clone of myself ▼
    change drumID ▼ by 1
```

Each drum is a different colour.

The drums are drawn around a circle.

Each clone will take the value of "drumID" from the original sprite when it's created.

Next drum

```
when I start as a clone
show
forever
    wait until     ChosenDrum = drumID
    change colour ▼ effect by 100
    wait until     not     ChosenDrum = drumID
    change colour ▼ effect by -100
```

Each drum runs this script.

15 The next script makes the drums light up as they play. Each clone waits for its unique ID to match the "ChosenDrum" variable. When it matches, a brief change in colour makes the drum appear to flash.

Wait for this drum's turn.

Wait for the turn to be over.

16 Run the project. The drums should light up in time to the sequence. Try the sequence "abcdefghijklmnopqrstuvwxyz" to see all the drums work in order and to see how the drums are reused after "r".

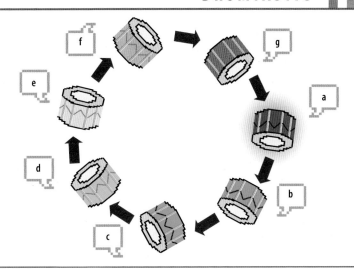

Hacks and tweaks

Being able to create a sequence that controls something is very useful. You could adapt this idea to make an automatic piano, singing ducks, or an on-screen robot that follows a program in the form of letter sequences.

▽ **Tempo**
The pace at which music plays is called its tempo. The higher the tempo, the shorter the beat and the faster the music. Scratch has a handy tempo setting – you'll find it in the Sound section of the blocks palette. Tick the tempo box to display it on stage. Add these scripts to the drum sprite so you can change the tempo with the arrow keys. The space-bar will reset the tempo to 60 beats per minute.

■ ■ **TRY THIS**

Word piano

If you change the "play drum" block to a "play note" block, you can create a singing animal. You'll need to set the total number of available notes to 26 so that every letter has its own note.

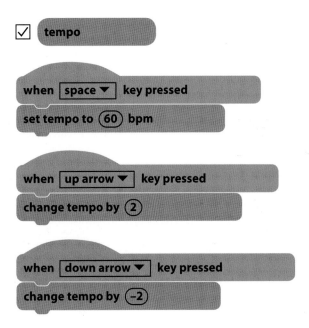

☑ tempo

when space ▼ key pressed
set tempo to (60) bpm

when up arrow ▼ key pressed
change tempo by (2)

when down arrow ▼ key pressed
change tempo by (-2)

Mindbenders

The Magic Spot

Run this project and stare at the cross in the middle while the pink spots around it flash on and off. Within a few seconds, a ghostly green spot will appear among the pink ones, but it isn't actually there. Scratch gets mysterious with this amazing optical illusion.

How it works

The spots take turns to disappear and reappear very quickly, causing a gap in the circle that races round. This confuses your brain, which fills in the missing spot with its opposite colour, creating a magic green spot that doesn't exist. Keep watching and the magic green spot will erase all the pink spots, but this is just an illusion too!

△ **Clones with identity**
Each circle is a clone. In this project, you'll see how each clone can have its own copy of a variable – in this case, an ID number that's used to control which circle is hidden at any moment.

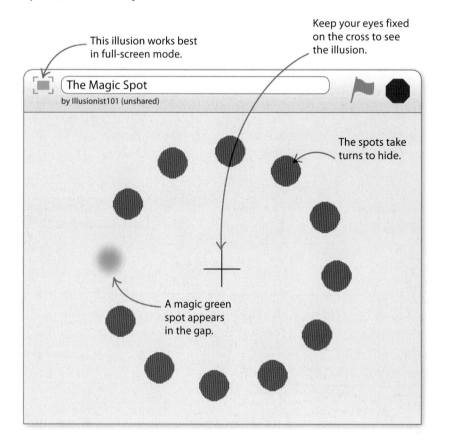

This illusion works best in full-screen mode.

Keep your eyes fixed on the cross to see the illusion.

The Magic Spot
by Illusionist101 (unshared)

The spots take turns to hide.

A magic green spot appears in the gap.

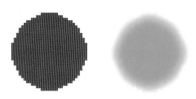

△ **Colour in your brain**
This kind of illusion is called an afterimage. If you stare at something for a long time without moving your eyes, the colour receptors in your eyes tire and your brain starts to tune colours out. So when the colour suddenly disappears, you briefly see a negative afterimage – a sort of "colour hole".

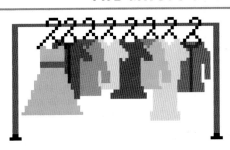

Pink costume

A single sprite is all that's needed to make this illusion, but first you'll need to draw the pink spot and black cross as costumes.

1 Start a new project and remove the cat sprite. Click on the paint symbol ✏ in the sprites list to draw a new sprite. Select the bright pink colour in the colour palette.

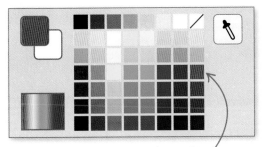

Make sure you choose this colour or the illusion might not work properly.

2 Select the ellipse tool and then, at the bottom of the paint editor, click on the right-hand oval to draw filled shapes rather than outlines.

Select this tool.

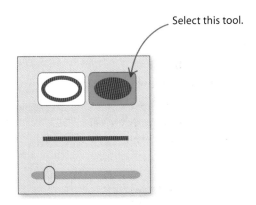

3 Click near the middle of the paint editor and drag the mouse while holding the shift key on the keyboard to paint a solid pink circle. Then release the mouse button and click outside the shape once to get rid of the box.

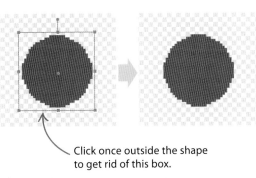

Click once outside the shape to get rid of this box.

4 Your newly drawn spot will appear in the costumes list. The numbers under its name tell you its size. You need a spot about 35x35 in size, but don't worry if it's wrong – the next step shows you how to resize it.

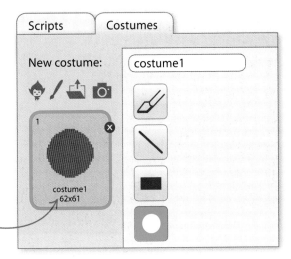

Scripts | Costumes

New costume: costume1

1

costume1
62x61

The numbers tell you the costume's size.

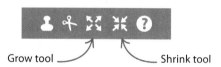

5 If it's too big or too small, click on either the shrink tool or grow tool at the top of the Scratch window. Click on the spot in the paint editor until the costume's size is 30–40.

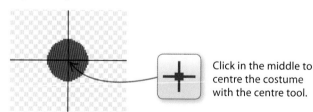

Grow tool ———→   ←——— Shrink tool

6 Click once more on the shrink or grow tool at the top to turn it off, then select the centre tool and click in the middle of your spot to centre it. Name this costume "Spot" at the top of the paint editor.

Click in the middle to centre the costume with the centre tool.

7 The next step is to create the black cross that appears in the middle of the illusion. Click the paint symbol **/** under the words "New costume" to start drawing a new costume, then use the line tool to make a black cross about half as big as the spot. To draw perfectly horizontal and straight lines, hold down the shift key. Centre the costume as you did with the spot.

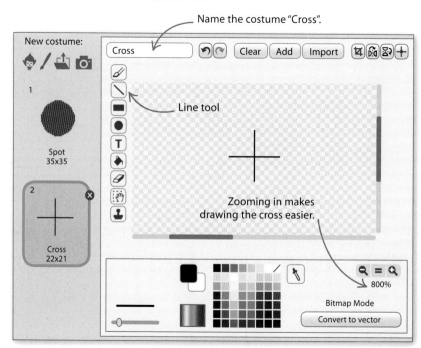

Name the costume "Cross".

New costume:

Cross

Line tool

Spot
35x35

Cross
22x21

Zooming in makes drawing the cross easier.

800%

Bitmap Mode
Convert to vector

Circle of clones

Now to fill in the background and create the circle of clones. The script will give each clone a unique identification number that will make it easy to hide.

8 To create the correct backdrop for the illusion, click on the paint symbol **/** in the lower left of Scratch.

Sprites

Stage
1 backdrop

Sprite1

New backdrop:

Click here to create a new backdrop.

9 Now select this grey colour. Make sure you get the exact shade or the illusion might not work properly. Use the fill tool ◆ to create a grey backdrop. Just click anywhere in the paint area.

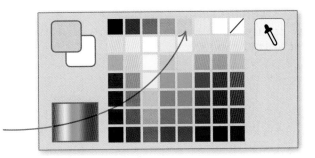

Make sure you select this shade of grey.

10 Click on the sprite and select the Scripts tab. Choose Data in the blocks palette and click on "Make a variable". Create a variable called "id" and select the option "For this sprite only". This is important as it allows each clone to have its own copy of the variable with its own value. Uncheck the tick box in the blocks palette so that the variable doesn't show on the stage.

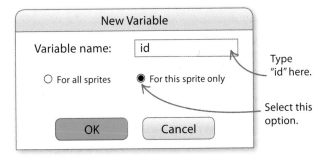

Type "id" here.

Select this option.

11 Now add the two scripts shown here to create 12 clones of the pink spot arranged in a circle. When a clone is created, it gets a copy of the original sprite's "id" variable, which means each clone has a unique number.

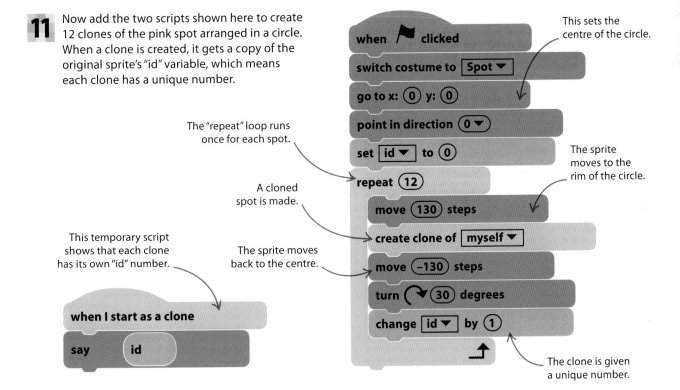

This sets the centre of the circle.

The "repeat" loop runs once for each spot.

A cloned spot is made.

The sprite moves to the rim of the circle.

This temporary script shows that each clone has its own "id" number.

The sprite moves back to the centre.

The clone is given a unique number.

12 Run the project and each clone will say its own value of "id". Each will be different, counting 0–11 around the circle.

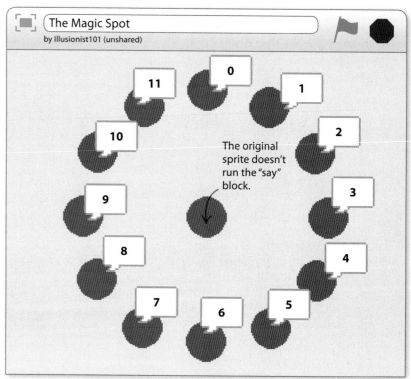

The original sprite doesn't run the "say" block.

13 Now delete the smaller script as you don't need to see those speech bubbles during the illusion.

Delete this script.

Creating the illusion

Now to make the code hide each of the spots in turn. You'll need to make a new variable, called "Hidden", that will specify which clone should hide.

14 Click the orange Data block in the blocks palette and make a new variable. Call it "Hidden". Uncheck its tick box in the blocks palette so that the variable doesn't appear on the stage.

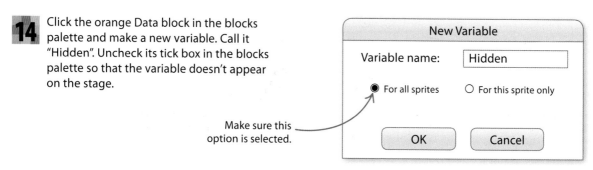

Make sure this option is selected.

15 Add the blocks shown below to the bottom of the sprite's script, but don't run the project yet.

16 Now add this separate script to the sprite. All the clones run this script. Only the clone whose "id" number matches the "Hidden" variable will hide. As the value of "Hidden" rises, each spot hides in turn.

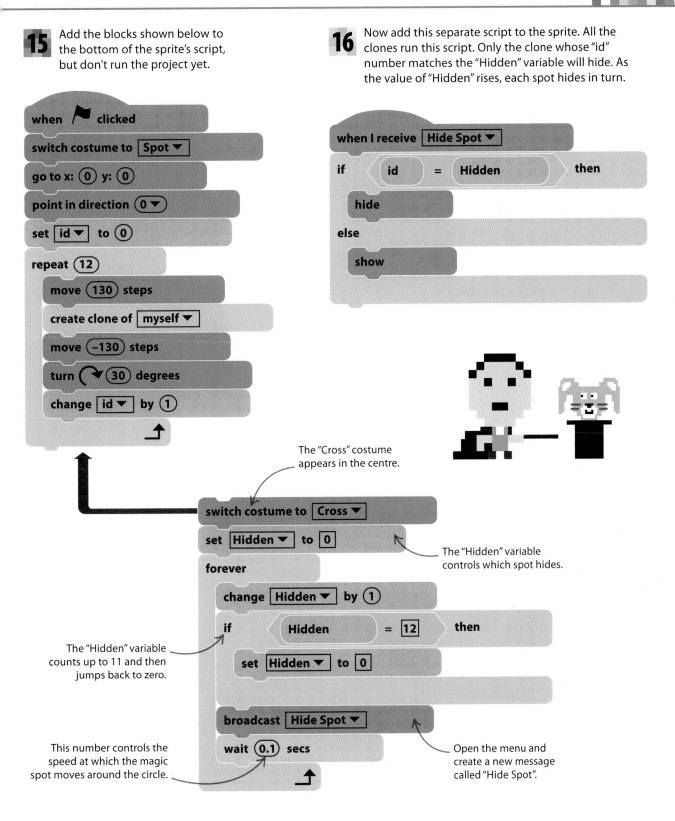

```
when 🏳 clicked
switch costume to Spot ▼
go to x: (0) y: (0)
point in direction (0 ▼)
set id ▼ to (0)
repeat (12)
    move (130) steps
    create clone of myself ▼
    move (-130) steps
    turn ↻ (30) degrees
    change id ▼ by (1)
```

```
when I receive Hide Spot ▼
if     id = Hidden      then
    hide
else
    show
```

The "Cross" costume appears in the centre.

```
switch costume to Cross ▼
set Hidden ▼ to (0)
forever
    change Hidden ▼ by (1)
    if     Hidden = 12      then
        set Hidden ▼ to (0)

    broadcast Hide Spot ▼
    wait (0.1) secs
```

The "Hidden" variable controls which spot hides.

The "Hidden" variable counts up to 11 and then jumps back to zero.

This number controls the speed at which the magic spot moves around the circle.

Open the menu and create a new message called "Hide Spot".

17 Run the project. You should see the gap move around the circle. Put the stage into full-screen mode and stare at the cross. Within a few seconds, you'll see the magic green spot. Keep staring at the cross and the magic spot will start to erase the pink spots. When you look away from the cross, you'll just see the empty gap again.

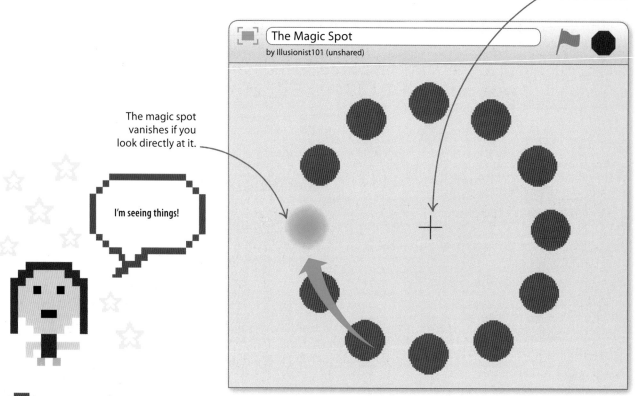

Stare at the cross to see the illusion.

The magic spot vanishes if you look directly at it.

I'm seeing things!

The Magic Spot
by Illusionist101 (unshared)

EXPERT TIPS

If then else

The "if then" block is very useful for either running or skipping a group of blocks depending on the answer to a question. But what if you want to do one thing for yes (true) and another for no (false)? You could use two "if then" blocks, but programmers face this problem so often that they created another solution: "if then else". The "if then else" block has two jaws, for two sets of blocks. The top set runs on yes, the bottom set runs on no.

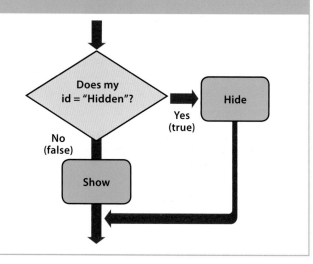

Hacks and tweaks

You can use Scratch to investigate this curious optical illusion further. Would the illusion still work if you change the colour of the spots or background or change the speed? What if there were more spots, or more than one spot hidden at the same time? The possibilities are endless. Save a copy and get fiddling with the code.

Right-click on the slider and set the minimum and maximum to –100 and 100.

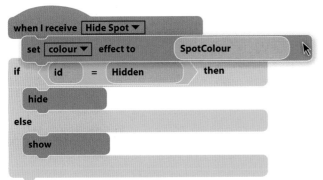

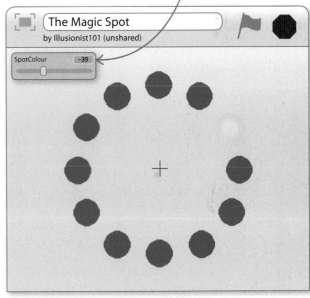

△ **Colour controls**

To find out which colours make the illusion strongest, create a new variable called "SpotColour" and add a slider to the stage. Add a "set colour effect" block to the sprite's script under the "when I receive" block. Run the project and try different colours. Which ones work best? Does the magic spot change colour too?

■ ■ **TRY THIS**

Speed it up

Try adding a new variable, called "Delay", to set the speed of the magic spot. You'll need to add these two blocks to the script – see if you can figure out where to put them. Right-click (or control/shift-click) on the variable on the stage and choose "slider". Does the illusion still work if you slow it right down?

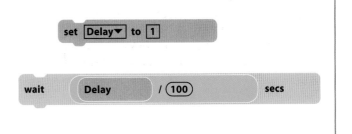

Spiral-o-tron

It's easy to use Scratch's Pen feature to create amazing visual effects, such as this multicoloured spinning spiral. If your computer has a microphone, you can adapt the project to make the spiral react to sound.

You can use a microphone to make the spiral move to the music!

How it works

There are many types of spiral, but this project paints a very simple one. Just take a step, turn 10 degrees to your right, take two steps, turn 10 degrees to your right, take three steps, and so on...

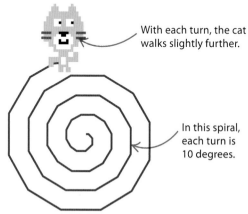

With each turn, the cat walks slightly further.

In this spiral, each turn is 10 degrees.

This project looks best in full-screen mode.

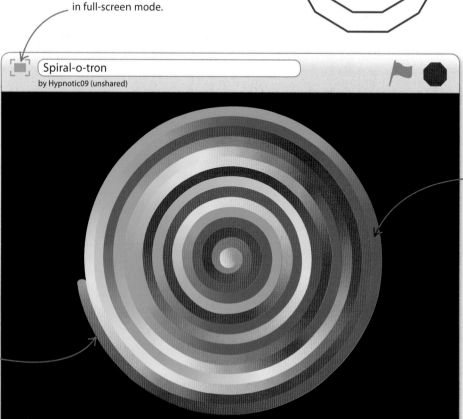

Spiral-o-tron
by Hypnotic09 (unshared)

The coloured line thickens in response to loud noises.

The spiral is drawn using the Scratch pen.

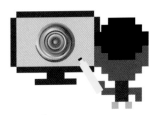

Build the spiral

This project shows you how to use Scratch's pen to create fast-moving, interactive effects. Follow the steps below to build a simple spiral first.

 1 Start a new project. Delete the cat sprite and click on the paint symbol ∕ in the sprites list. You don't need to draw a sprite as it's just a guide for the pen. Call the sprite "Spiral".

Spiral

2 Now turn the stage black to make the spiral stand out. Click on the backdrop's paint symbol ∕ in the lower left of Scratch. Pick black in the paint editor and use the fill tool to create a solid black backdrop.

Use the fill tool to colour the backdrop.

3 The project needs lots of variables. Select the spiral sprite and create the following variables: "Repeats", "DrawLength", "DrawLengthIncrease", "TurnAngle", and "StartDirection". Untick their check boxes so they don't appear on the stage.

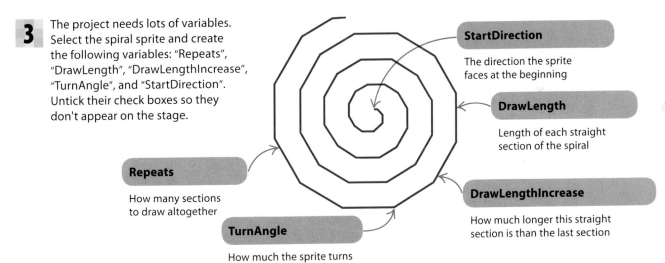

StartDirection
The direction the sprite faces at the beginning

DrawLength
Length of each straight section of the spiral

DrawLengthIncrease
How much longer this straight section is than the last section

Repeats
How many sections to draw altogether

TurnAngle
How much the sprite turns

4 Now create a custom block to draw a spiral. Select More Blocks and then click on "Make a Block".

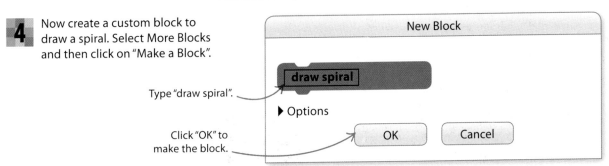

New Block

draw spiral

▶ Options

Type "draw spiral".

Click "OK" to make the block.

OK   Cancel

5 You will now see the "define draw spiral" header in the scripts area. Add the following script to it. Read through the Scratch blocks and think about the steps. Don't run the project yet as there isn't any code to trigger the new block.

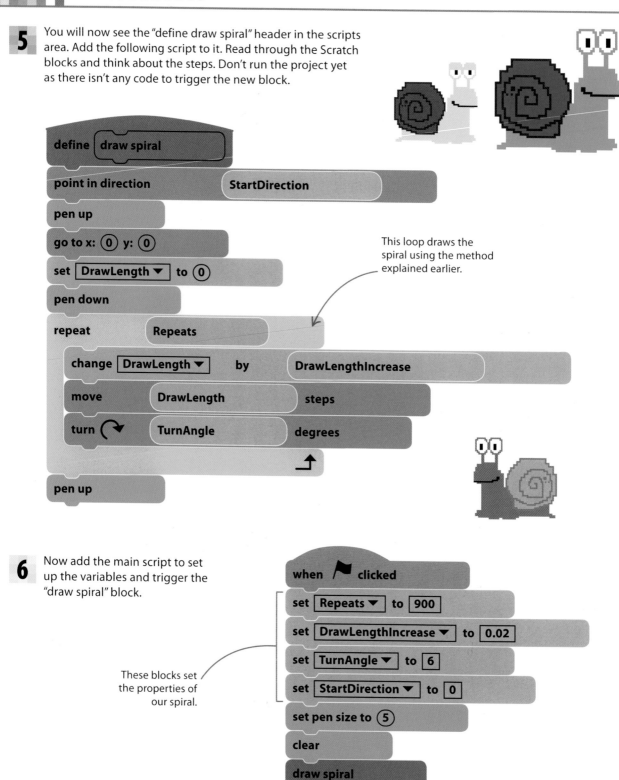

define draw spiral

point in direction StartDirection

pen up

go to x: 0 y: 0

set DrawLength ▼ to 0

pen down

repeat Repeats

change DrawLength ▼ by DrawLengthIncrease

move DrawLength steps

turn ↻ TurnAngle degrees

pen up

This loop draws the spiral using the method explained earlier.

6 Now add the main script to set up the variables and trigger the "draw spiral" block.

when 🏴 clicked

set Repeats ▼ to 900

set DrawLengthIncrease ▼ to 0.02

set TurnAngle ▼ to 6

set StartDirection ▼ to 0

set pen size to 5

clear

draw spiral

These blocks set the properties of our spiral.

7 Run the project. A spiral like this will appear. It will take around 30 seconds to draw.

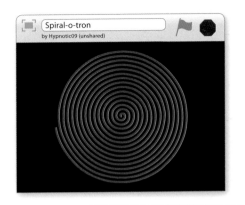

Spin the spiral

To make the spiral spin, Scratch will draw it repeatedly, each time in a new position. To make this happen quickly, you need to use a special trick to run blocks faster.

8 The spiral takes a long time to draw because Scratch redraws the whole stage every time you add a new straight-line section to the spiral. You can set the custom block to not redraw the spiral until it's finished. To do this, right-click on the "define" block and choose "edit".

9 Now click on "Options" and the menu shown below will appear. Tick the box labelled "Run without screen refresh".

Click here to open the options menu.

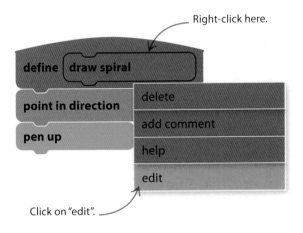

Right-click here.

Click on "edit".

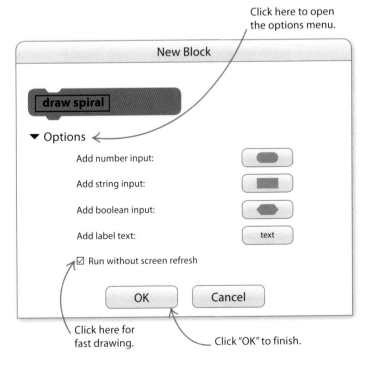

Click here for fast drawing.

Click "OK" to finish.

10 Now run the project and the spiral will appear so quickly that you won't see it happen. The next trick is to keep redrawing the spiral in different positions so it appears to spin. Add a new variable called "SpinSpeed", untick its box, and change the main script to look like this.

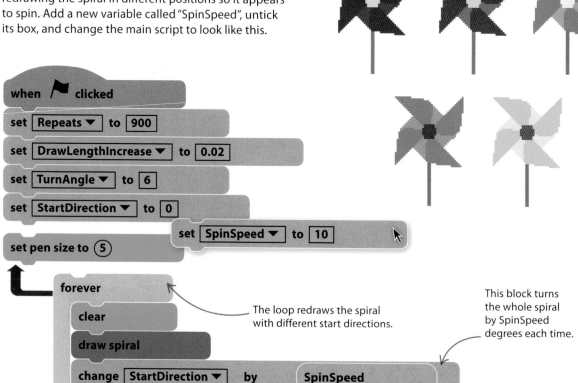

when ⚑ clicked

set Repeats ▼ to 900

set DrawLengthIncrease ▼ to 0.02

set TurnAngle ▼ to 6

set StartDirection ▼ to 0

set SpinSpeed ▼ to 10

set pen size to 5

forever
  clear
  draw spiral
  change StartDirection ▼ by SpinSpeed

The loop redraws the spiral with different start directions.

This block turns the whole spiral by SpinSpeed degrees each time.

11 Run the project and watch the spiral spin. Try switching to full-screen mode for a hypnotic effect. If you stare at the centre for a while and then look away, you might see things ripple weirdly for a moment – an optical illusion.

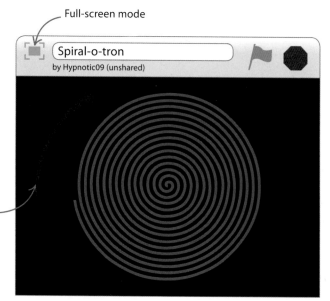

Full-screen mode

Spiral-o-tron
by Hypnotic09 (unshared)

The whole spiral spins clockwise.

Add some colour

The pen colour can be controlled to create some amazing effects. Simple changes to the scripts create patterns like the one shown here.

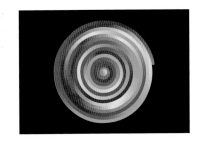

12 Add another variable: "ColourChange". Then change the scripts as shown here and run them to see the new colourful spiral.

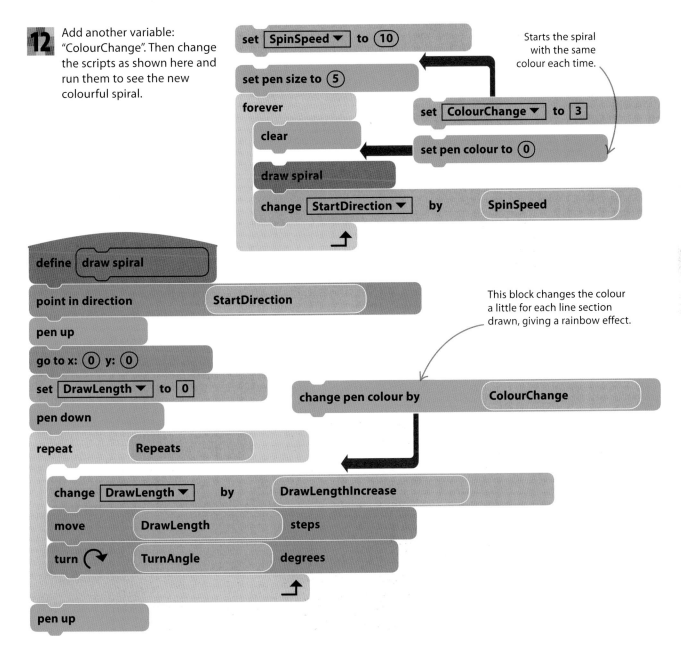

```
set SpinSpeed ▼ to (10)

set pen size to (5)

forever
    clear
    draw spiral
    change StartDirection ▼ by SpinSpeed
```

Starts the spiral with the same colour each time.

```
set ColourChange ▼ to 3

set pen colour to (0)
```

```
define draw spiral

point in direction       StartDirection

pen up

go to x: (0) y: (0)

set DrawLength ▼ to 0

pen down

repeat          Repeats

    change DrawLength ▼ by       DrawLengthIncrease
    move       DrawLength          steps
    turn ↻     TurnAngle          degrees

pen up
```

```
change pen colour by          ColourChange
```

This block changes the colour a little for each line section drawn, giving a rainbow effect.

Move to the music

If your computer has a microphone, you can make the spiral react to sounds and music. You'll need to use special blocks that detect and measure sound volume.

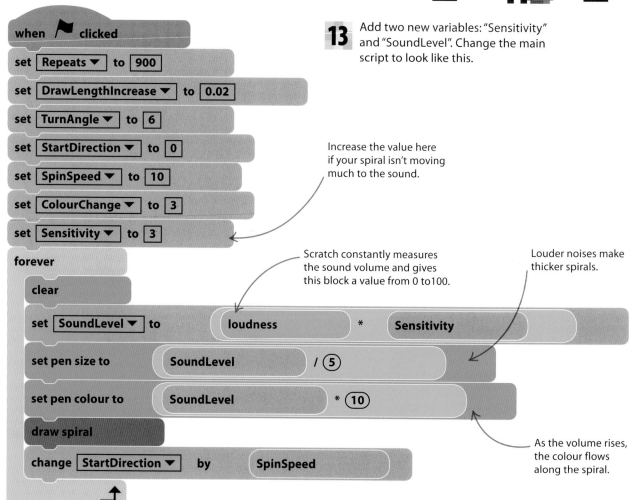

```
when [flag] clicked
set Repeats to 900
set DrawLengthIncrease to 0.02
set TurnAngle to 6
set StartDirection to 0
set SpinSpeed to 10
set ColourChange to 3
set Sensitivity to 3
forever
    clear
    set SoundLevel to (loudness * Sensitivity)
    set pen size to (SoundLevel / 5)
    set pen colour to (SoundLevel * 10)
    draw spiral
    change StartDirection by SpinSpeed
```

13 Add two new variables: "Sensitivity" and "SoundLevel". Change the main script to look like this.

Increase the value here if your spiral isn't moving much to the sound.

Scratch constantly measures the sound volume and gives this block a value from 0 to100.

Louder noises make thicker spirals.

As the volume rises, the colour flows along the spiral.

14 Run the project and play some music or sing near your computer. Scratch will ask you to use your microphone – it's OK to click "yes". The spiral will dance to the music!

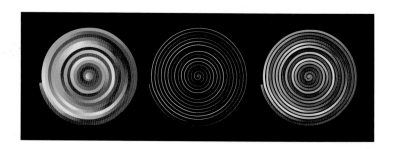

Hacks and tweaks

Don't be afraid to change the variables or other numbers in the code to see what happens. You can also add slider controls to experiment with the look and motion of the spiral.

▽ **Sliders**

If you show the control variables on the stage, you can right-click and add sliders to them. These allow you to experiment with different values while the project is running.

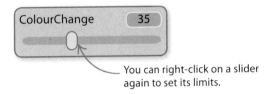

You can right-click on a slider again to set its limits.

▽ **Presets**

If you use your sliders to make a spiral you really like, write down all the values and then create a "preset" to set those values at the touch of a key.

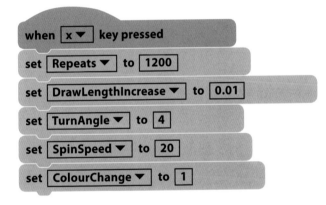

▽ **Hiders**

You can add scripts like these to show and hide your sliders when you hit certain keys. That way they won't spoil the view!

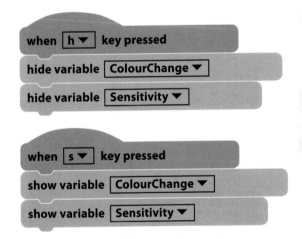

```
· · TRY THIS
```
Sound reaction

You can have a lot of fun in other projects making sprites react to sound. Tick the "loudness" block to see the volume displayed on the stage. Try giving scripts like these to some sprites or invent your own scripts.

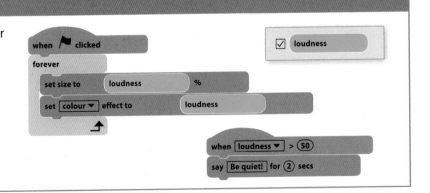

What next?

Next steps

After working through this book, your knowledge of Scratch should be strong enough to take you to new places. Here's some advice on taking your coding skills to the next level, as well as a few suggestions on where to find inspiration for your own projects.

Exploring Scratch

The Scratch website **www.scratch.mit.edu** is a great place to see other people's work and share your own projects. Click "Explore" at the top of the website to view projects that other Scratchers have shared.

There are millions of projects on the Scratch website. Click here to see what great stuff you can find.

Click the Studios tab to see projects grouped by themes that Scratchers have created.

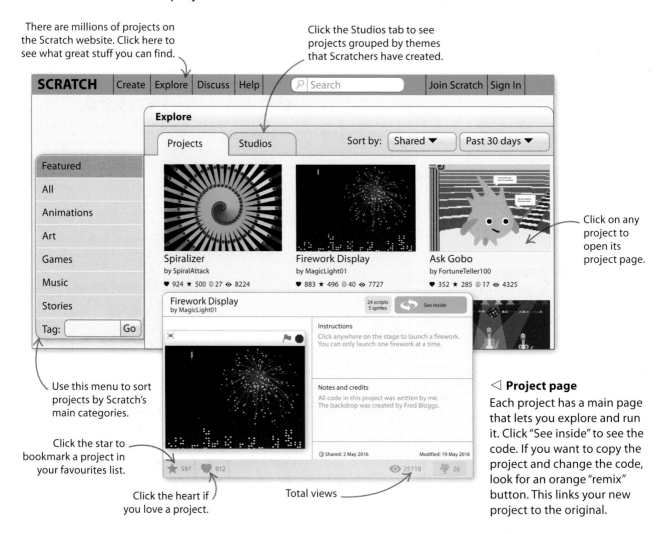

Click on any project to open its project page.

Use this menu to sort projects by Scratch's main categories.

Click the star to bookmark a project in your favourites list.

Click the heart if you love a project.

Total views

◁ **Project page**
Each project has a main page that lets you explore and run it. Click "See inside" to see the code. If you want to copy the project and change the code, look for an orange "remix" button. This links your new project to the original.

▷ **Sharing**

To share one of your projects with other Scratchers, open the project and click the "Share" button at the top of Scratch. Anyone can find your project once you've shared it. You can also see how many fellow Scratchers have tried your projects, and people can "favourite" and "love" your project too.

Making your own projects

Scratch is a great playground for trying out your own coding ideas. Open up a new project and see where your computer mouse takes you.

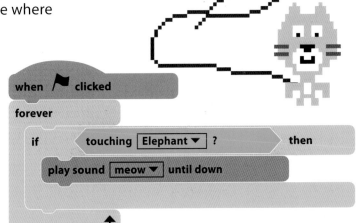

▽ **Doodling**

Scratch is designed to make experimenting easy. Just add a sprite you like and create some fun scripts like these. Maybe turn on the pen to see what loopy pattern your sprite makes. Play with variables and add sliders so you can see their effects immediately.

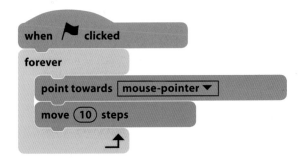

▽ **Have fun!**

Programming can be great fun. Working with others and sharing your projects will really help your coding develop. Why not join or start a code club at your school or local library? Or get together with friends who like Scratch and have a coding party where you can work on themed projects together.

▽ **Learn another language**

Why not stretch yourself and learn another programming language? Python is easy to get started in, and you'll recognize many of the techniques used in Scratch, like making decisions using "if then" and repeating code with loops.

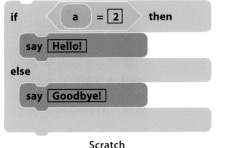

```
if a == 2:
    print('Hello!')
else:
    print('Goodbye!')
```

Scratch   Python

Glossary

algorithm
A set of step-by-step instructions that perform a task. Computer programs are based on algorithms.

animation
Changing pictures quickly to create the illusion of movement.

backpack
A storage area in Scratch that allows you to copy things between projects.

bitmap graphics
Computer drawings stored as a grid of pixels. Compare with *vector graphics*.

block
An instruction in Scratch that can be joined to other blocks to build a script.

Boolean expression
A statement that is either true or false, leading to two possible outcomes. Boolean blocks in Scratch are hexagonal rather than rounded.

branch
A point in a program where two different options are available, such as the "if then else" block in Scratch.

bug
A coding error that makes a program behave in an unexpected way.

call
To use a function, procedure, or subprogram. A custom block in Scratch is a call to the "define" script with the same name.

clone
A fully functioning copy of a sprite that can move and run scripts on its own, separate from the original sprite.

condition
A "true or false" statement used to make a decision in a program. See also *Boolean expression*.

coordinates
A pair of numbers that pinpoint an exact spot on the stage. Usually written as (x, y).

costume
The picture a sprite shows on the stage. Rapidly changing a sprite's costume can create an animation.

data
Information, such as text, symbols, or numbers.

debug
To look for and correct errors in a program.

directory
A place to store files to keep them organized.

ellipse
An oval

event
Something a computer program can react to, such as a key being pressed or the mouse being clicked.

execute
See *run*

export
To send something to the computer from Scratch, such as a sprite or a whole project saved as a computer file.

file
A collection of data stored with a name.

fractal
A pattern or shape that looks the same when you zoom in or out, such as the shape of a cloud, a tree, or a cauliflower.

function
Code that carries out a specific task, working like a program within a program. Also called a procedure, subprogram, or subroutine.

global variable
A variable that can be changed and used by any sprite in a project.

gradient (colour)
Moving smoothly from one colour to another, like the sky during a beautiful sunset.

graphics
Visual elements on a screen that are not text, such as pictures, icons, and symbols.

GUI
The GUI, or graphical user interface, is the name for the buttons and windows that make up the part of the program you can see and interact with.

hack
An ingenious change to code that makes it do something new or simplifies it. (Also, accessing a computer without permission.)

hardware
The physical parts of a computer that you can see or touch, such as wires, the keyboard, and the screen.

header block
A Scratch block that starts a script, such as the "when green flag clicked" block. Also known as a hat block.

import
To bring something in from outside Scratch, such as a picture or sound clip from the computer's files.

index number
A number given to an item in a list.

input
Data that is entered into a computer. Keyboards, mice, and microphones can be used to input data.

integer
A whole number. An integer does not contain a decimal point and is not written as a fraction.

interface
See *GUI*

library
A collection of sprites, costumes, or sounds that can be used in Scratch programs.

list
A collection of items stored in a numbered order.

local variable
A variable that can be changed by only one sprite. Each copy or clone of a sprite has its own separate version of the variable.

loop
A part of a program that repeats itself, removing the need to type out the same piece of code multiple times.

memory
A computer chip inside a computer that stores data.

message
A way to send information between sprites.

network
A group of interconnected computers that exchange data. The internet is a giant network.

operating system (OS)
The program that controls everything on a computer, such as Windows, OS X, or Linux.

operator
A Scratch block that uses data to work something out, such as checking whether two values are equal or adding two numbers together.

output
Data that is produced by a computer program and viewed by the user.

particle effect
A visual effect in which lots of small patterns move in an organized way to create a larger pattern. Particle effects in Scratch usually use clones.

physics
The science of how things move and affect each other. Including physics is often important in simulations and games – for example, to create realistic gravity.

pixel art
A drawing made of giant pixels or blocks, mimicking the appearance of graphics in early computer games.

pixels
The coloured dots on a screen that make up graphics.

procedure
Code that carries out a specific task, working like a program within a program. Also called a function, subprogram, or subroutine.

program
A set of instructions that a computer follows in order to complete a task.

programming language
A language that is used to give instructions to a computer.

project
Scratch's name for a program and all the sprites, sounds, and backdrops that go with it.

Python
A popular programming language created by Guido van Rossum. Python is a great language to learn after Scratch.

random
A function in a computer program that allows unpredictable outcomes. Useful when creating games.

run
The command to make a program start.

Scratcher
Someone who uses Scratch.

script
A stack of instruction blocks under a header block that are run in order.

server
A computer that stores files accessible via a network.

simulation
A realistic imitation of something. A weather simulator might re-create the action of wind, rain, and snow.

software
Programs that run on a computer and control how it works.

sprite
A picture on the stage in Scratch that a script can move and change.

stage
The screen-like area of the Scratch interface in which projects run.

statement
The smallest complete instruction a programming language can be broken down into.

string
A series of characters. Strings can contain numbers, letters, or symbols.

subprogram or subroutine
Code that carries out a specific task, working like a program within a program. Also called a function or procedure.

turbo mode
A way of running Scratch projects that makes the code work much faster than normal. You can switch turbo mode on and off by holding the shift key as you click the green flag.

tweak
A small change made to something to make it work better or differently.

variable
A place to store data that can change in a program, such as the player's score. A variable has a name and a value.

vector graphics
Computer drawings stored as collections of shapes, making them easier to change. Compare with *bitmap graphics*.

Index

Page numbers in **bold** refer to main entries.

Acknowledgments

Dorling Kindersley would like to thank Caroline Hunt for proofreading;
Helen Peters for the index; Sean Ross for help with Scratch; Ira Pundeer
for editorial assistance; Nishwan Rasool for picture research assistance;
and Vishal Bhatia for pre-production assistance.

Jon Woodcock would like to thank all his code clubbers over the
years for teaching him how to think in Scratch; and Matty and Amy
for all their questions.

Scratch is developed by the Lifelong Kindergarten Group at MIT
Media Lab. See **http://scratch.mit.edu**

The publisher would like to thank the following for their kind
permission to reproduce their photographs:

(Key: a-above; b-below/bottom; c-centre; f-far; l-left; r-right; t-top)

134 123RF.com: Jacek Chabraszewski (b); **Dreamstime.com**: Pavel Losevsky
(b/background); **163 Corbis**: Trizeps Photography / photocuisine (cra); **NASA**:
(cr); **Science Photo Library**: SUSUMU NISHINAGA (crb); **173 NOAA**: (tr)

All other images © Dorling Kindersley
For further information see: **www.dkimages.com**